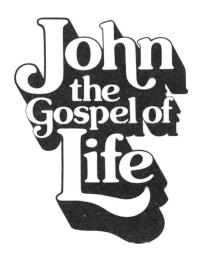

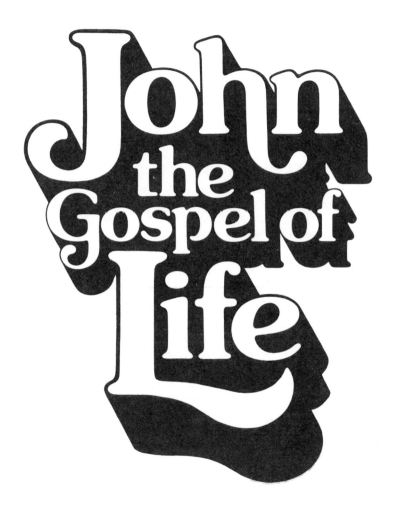

John the Gospel of Life

D. GEORGE VANDERLIP

Judson Press ® Valley Forge

JOHN: THE GOSPEL OF LIFE

Copyright © 1979
Judson Press, Valley Forge, PA 19482-0851
Fourth Printing, 1988

Unless otherwise indicated, Bible quotations in this volume are in accordance with the *New American Standard Bible,* © The Lockman Foundation 1960, 1962, 1963, 1968, 1971, 1972, 1973, 1975, and are used by permission.

Other versions of the Bible quoted in this book are:

Today's English Version, *Good News for Modern Man,* Copyright © American Bible Society, 1966.

The New English Bible with the Apocrypha, Copyright © The Delegates of the Oxford University Press and The Syndics of the Cambridge University Press, 1961, 1970.

The New Testament in the Language of the People by Charles B. Williams. Copyright © 1965, 1966 by Edith S Williams. Used by permission of Moody Press, The Moody Bible Institute of Chicago.

Weymouth's New Testament in Modern Speech by Richard Francis Weymouth. Reprinted by permission of Harper & Row, Publishers, Inc.

The Holy Bible, King James Version.

The Revised Standard Version of the Bible, copyrighted 1946, 1952, 1971, 1973 © by the Division of Christian Education of the National Council of the Churches of Christ in the United States of America, and used by permission.

Library of Congress Cataloging in Publication Data
Vanderlip, George.
  John, the Gospel of life.

  Bibliography: p.
  Includes index.
  1. Bible. N. T. John—Criticism, interpretation, etc. I. Title.
BS2615.2.V37   226'.5'07   78-25884
ISBN 0-8170-0826-8

Dedicated to our son

JOHN

Foreword

The Fourth Gospel has been of perennial interest to scholars and to the rank and file of Christians for centuries. Its message of eternal life through Jesus Christ, fortified by signs of his divine-human nature and a clear proclamation of his triumph over sin and death, has provided comfort and assurance to countless generations of believers.

To the already vast library of books and commentaries written to interpret this Gospel According to John, Dr. D. George Vanderlip has added this collection of ten very readable and impressive chapters under the title *John: The Gospel of Life*. The great themes of the Fourth Evangelist are given a fresh interpretation within the perspective of the Gospel's dual purpose: to demonstrate that Jesus is the promised Messiah of Israel (chapters 1-12) and to deepen the faith of Christians (chapters 13-21).

Out of a wide experience as a seminary professor and biblical scholar, Dr. Vanderlip never loses sight of the Evangelist's focus "on Jesus as the one who came to bring life and light to humanity" so that, "in following him, the hungry find bread, the thirsty find drink, the blind find sight, the captives find freedom, and the spiritually dead find eternal life." His interpretation is especially appropriate for modern readers, for he relates the gospel message to both personal and social needs that call for a balanced attention in our day.

Dr. Vanderlip combines skills in biblical exegesis with theological insights which result in a book that presents a Gospel that "lifts our vision from the restrictions of the world of time and space of God's eternity." Just a few examples may be cited for illustration.

In chapter 4, entitled "From Death to Life," he ties the miracle of new wine, the cleansing of the temple, and the conversations with Nicodemus and the woman of Samaria together with a consistent theme of "newness," or of something "better" which had replaced what was formerly present and inferior. In chapter 5 he uses three different images (Jesus as the bread of life, John 6; Jesus as the water of life, John 7; Jesus as the light of life, John 8) to symbolize the truth that Jesus is the Source of life.

Under the title of "Life Transformed," chapter 7 interprets John 13 and 14. Particularly interesting is the observation that Jesus' washing of his disciples' feet is a prediction and symbol of their ultimate cleansing from their sins through his death on the cross. In chapter 8, entitled "Life in Christ," Dr. Vanderlip gathers together the symbol of the vine as stressing the organic unity of the church (John 15), the role of the Holy Spirit in providing a new quality of life (John 16), and the high priestly prayer that tells us the meaning of eternal life and stresses the unity of the church (John 17).

In chapter 9, "Life Through Death," the author directs attention to the tendency of John's Gospel to minimize Pilate's involvement in the death of Jesus and thus to place the fuller burden for the crucifixion on the Jews. He warns Christians against indulging in an anti-Semitic generalization that all Jews are "Christ-killers" and therefore totally rejected by God. This attitude is a consequence of failing to distinguish between those who were directly responsible for the crucifixion, both Jewish leaders and Roman authorities, and the many Jews who were either openly followers of Jesus or at least refrained from being a party to his death.

The final chapter, "Life Proclaimed," is a firm affirmation of the resurrection of Jesus as central in the message of the early church, and of Christ's gift of the Holy Spirit as the source of a new quality of life that brings joy, peace, and hope.

Dr. Vanderlip has produced a most readable and convincing interpretation of the Gospel According to John. His own deep devotion to its message shines through his writing. The care with which he has sifted the varied views of scholars regarding the unique character of this Fourth Gospel, its date of writing in the light of the Dead Sea Scrolls, and its authorship provides for pastors and lay readers a valuable background for study which is up to date and conservatively appraised. This reason, combined with the author's timely exposition of the themes of this Gospel, affords adequate justification for the publication of yet another book to shed light on this favorite Gospel of the church.

Robert G. Torbet

Preface

This interpretation of the Gospel According to John finds as the central theme the affirmation that in Jesus Christ is life (1:4). He is the source of life's true meaning and the one who can give to us life "in all its fullness" (10:10, NEB). This analysis of the Gospel According to John moves through the Gospel in a systematic fashion. At the same time, it seeks throughout to apply John's message to contemporary personal and social concerns.

To Dr. Robert G. Torbet I express heartfelt thanks both for the writing of the Foreword and for his warm friendship over several years. I wish also to give thanks to Mrs. Culbert G. (Duron) Rutenber for preparing the manuscript for publication. To the Reverend Alden G. Dick I am indebted for a number of helpful suggestions while the book was being written. Finally, I wish to acknowledge with appreciation permission granted by Judson Press to include some material which appeared in another form in the *Baptist Leader* magazine.

The preparation of this book has been a joy because it has exposed me once more to the rich spiritual food which is to be found in John and which nourishes some of the deepest needs in the lives of all of us. It is my hope that this presentation of John's portrayal of spiritual life may bring inner refreshment and renewal to each and every reader.

D. George Vanderlip

Eastern Baptist Theological Seminary
Philadelphia, Pennsylvania
March 1, 1978

Contents

The Gospel of Life

The Eagle's View

Our New Testament opens with four different Gospels. Each one of them tells the story about Jesus of Nazareth. All of them agree in affirming that Jesus is the Son of God and that he is the Savior for all humankind. Yet each Gospel contains a distinctive account of what Jesus said and taught. Each of the Gospels has a special emphasis. The Gospel According to John portrays Jesus in such a majestic manner that artists through the centuries have represented John and his record of the life of Jesus with the symbol of the eagle. This majestic bird with powerful, outstretched wings, telescopic sight, and royal bearing is a proper image for the beauty, dignity, and power of John's account of the life and teachings of Jesus. What book of the Bible can be compared to it? It is like the large sparkling center diamond on a diamond ring with several smaller diamonds alongside it. This Gospel lifts our vision from the restrictions of the world of time and space to God's eternity. Whereas Mark begins his Gospel with Jesus at thirty years of age and Matthew and Luke begin with his birth in Bethlehem, John begins before creation itself. "In the beginning was the Word" (1:1), and "the Word became flesh" (1:14), namely, Jesus of Nazareth.

15

Throughout the centuries people have found in the Gospel According to John spiritual food to nourish the deepest longings of the human heart. Young and old alike have found in it guidance for living. This Gospel centers on Jesus as the one who came to bring life and light to humanity. In following him, the hungry find bread, the thirsty find drink, the blind find sight, the captives find freedom, and the spiritually dead find eternal life. This Gospel radiates with hope and joy, and as it is read, the river of life continues to flow into the hearts of its readers.

Why Was John Written?

In the following passage the writer tells us why he wrote his Gospel: "Many other signs therefore Jesus also performed in the presence of the disciples, which are not written in this book; but these have been written that you may believe that Jesus is the Christ, the Son of God; and that believing you may have life in his name" (20:30-31). In this statement we are told three important facts:

1. Jesus is the Christ, the Son of God. The central purpose of this Gospel is to tell us about him. The word "Christ" is a title. It comes from the Greek word *Christos,* which means "Anointed One," and it is a translation of the Hebrew word "Messiah," which has the same meaning. John wrote in order to demonstrate that Jesus was the promised Messiah of Israel. The Messiah was the one anointed by God whose coming was foretold by the Hebrew prophets. In popular expectation the Messiah would deliver Israel from its bondage to political enemies. He came, however, to do an even greater work than that. He came to deliver all persons from the bondage of sin.

2. The second affirmation has to do with our response to Jesus Christ. The Gospel was written to lead its readers to "believe" in him. This response means much more than an intellectual acceptance of certain doctrines about Jesus. It means trust, commitment, and a personal, life-transforming relationship.

3. The third statement is a promise, namely, that when we do believe in Jesus as the Christ, we will receive "life." The entire Gospel is really an explanation of what the word "life" means.

There are two words for "life" in Greek—*bios* and *zoe. Bios* means physical life or existence. People share this with the animals. *Zoe,* as John uses it, means spiritual life. It is best defined as a relationship or fellowship with the Creator. John tells us what he means by life when he quotes Jesus in his prayer as saying, "And this is eternal life, that they may know Thee, the only true God, and Jesus Christ whom Thou hast sent" (17:3). The word "know" in this verse does not refer to intellectual comprehension but to fellowship, communion, and obedience. Jesus defines his one purpose for coming into the world in terms of life. He said, "I came that they might have life, and might have it abundantly" (10:10b). *The New English Bible* renders this verse in a helpful way when it writes, "I have come that men may have life, and may have it *in all its fullness*" (italics added). Jesus came not to impoverish or restrict our lives but to expand and to enrich them. The word "abundantly" can be translated "overflowing." God desires that our cup of life overflow. Joy, peace, meaning, purpose, fulfillment—all of these qualities are part of what is implied when Jesus says that he came in order that we might have life and have it abundantly.

Jesus, the Light of the World

The Gospel According to John was written because the writer was convinced that Jesus is the light for living. He says in the opening paragraph of his work, "In Him was life; and the life was the light of men" (1:4). Later he quotes Jesus' words, "I am the light of the world; he who follows Me shall not walk in the darkness, but shall have the light of life" (8:12).

Light is something which can either reassure or frighten. Light sometimes means destruction. When the atomic bombs fell over Hiroshima and Nagasaki, great fireballs mounted to the sky, and below them many thousands died. This past summer I visited Pompeii, the city which was destroyed in A.D. 79 by the fiery eruption of Mount Vesuvius. In one day this flourishing Italian resort town with its wealthy villas was covered with cinders and ashes. For Pompeii's first-century inhabitants the fire and light from Vesuvius meant death and destruction.

On one occasion my family and I were vacationing in Ocean City, New Jersey. One evening my wife and I were enjoying the boardwalk when unexpectedly the sky became dark and the wind mounted. Lightning flashed in the distance, and it was announced that an electrical storm was approaching. We set out immediately to walk the three blocks to the place where we were staying. We walked briskly, but the faster we moved, the more the elements threatened. The sky continued to darken, the lightning came closer and closer, and soon the rain began to fall in large drops around us. We quickened our pace. With each flash of lightning the thunder became more intense. We had hardly made it safely inside our residence when the brightest flash of all lit up the sky. It was accompanied by a thunderclap so loud that it was painful to the ears. We discovered that that bright lightning bolt had struck the house directly across the street from us. Several bricks were dislodged from a chimney, and these cascaded down the peaked roof to the sidewalk below. Fortunately no fire followed. In a short time the storm was over. While it lasted, however, the flashing brightness of the lightning and the loudness of the thunder was anything but reassuring.

On the other hand, the presence of light can be a most welcome experience. Once when we were flying to Israel, as we were approaching the coast, the pilot of our plane turned out the interior lights of the aircraft in order that we might see the lights of Tel Aviv and of the Ben Gurion Airport. How welcome those lights must have been to any Jewish immigrants on board who were coming at last to their "homeland"!

Some years ago it was my privilege to be in the home of Rabbi Isaac Nissim, the chief rabbi of Israel. There were about twenty of us in the party; most of us were college or seminary teachers. At one point Rabbi Nissim asked through an interpreter why we had come to Israel. A member of our group responded without hesitation with a quotation from the Old Testament. He said, "We have come to Israel because we believe the word of Isaiah who said, 'I will make you a light to the nations'" (Isaiah 49:6b, NEB). The rabbi's face gleamed, and his eyes sparkled; he was obviously pleased by the response he had received. How much more can we as believers in Jesus as the Savior affirm these words about Jesus Christ! He is a light to the nations. We who have believed in him know the truth of the words expressed in the Gospel According to John when Jesus said, "He who follows Me shall not walk in the darkness, but shall have the light of life" (John 8:12). In Jesus, God's promise through Isaiah has been fulfilled: "I will make you a light to the nations, to be my salvation to earth's farthest bounds" (Isaiah 49:6b, NEB).

For Whom Did John Write?

Did John write for Christians in order to deepen their faith or for persons whom he desired to evangelize? The book which he wrote can serve both purposes very well, and it has done so through the years.

Parts of John are especially concerned with demonstrating that Jesus is the promised Messiah of Israel. This is especially true of chapters 1 through 12. Chapters 13 through 21 are centered almost exclusively on Christian instruction. At the time that John wrote the book, believers were involved in an ongoing debate with leaders of the Jewish synagogues concerning the Christians' claims that Jesus was the Messiah. Chapters 1 through 12 reflect some of these debates, and they may have been included in the Gospel in order to help Christian readers in their responsibility as witnesses to Jesus Christ. While John wrote his Gospel primarily to instruct the church, the concern for evangelism burned very brightly in his heart. Consequently, the Gospel can be used both to deepen the understanding and commitment of believers and to explain in clear and unambiguous terms what it means to become a disciple of Jesus Christ. Both concerns flow through this Gospel.

When Was John Written?

Scholarship tends to date John much earlier today than it did a few decades ago. We actually have a fragment of a copy of John, known as P52, which has been dated from about A.D. 125. This fragment contains John 18:31-34 on one side and John 18:37-38 on the other. A complete copy of the Gospel According to John which is dated around A.D. 200 was published for the first time in 1956 and 1958. This is known as the Bodmer Papyrus II, or P66.

Some scholars today tend to date part or all of John before A.D. 70. Others prefer a date for John around A.D. 85–90. Perhaps both dates have merit if, as some have suggested, the Gospel was first written in a shorter edition and subsequently expanded.

There appears to be a reference to the death of Peter in John 21:18-19 as an event which had already taken place. When the book was written, the author could understand the statement of Jesus about what would happen to Peter because Peter's death had already occurred. Since this happened about A.D. 65, we must date chapter 21 after that time. Some interpreters have also seen an indirect reference to the death of the beloved disciple in this same chapter. In any case, the final chapter of John may be regarded as an epilogue to the book. One solution to the problem of dating may lie in the suggestion made above that the Gospel went through more than one stage of writing. The early development would be before A.D. 70 and the full Gospel would have been completed around A.D. 85–90.

Who Wrote the Gospel?

The strength of the early tradition which ascribes this Gospel to John the apostle, combined with many geographically accurate references in this Gospel, reinforces the argument that the witness of John, the son of Zebedee, stands behind this Gospel. There appears to be a "Johannine circle," that is to say, a group of persons who have been influenced by John and his thought, and perhaps these individuals are referred to by the pronoun "we" in John 21:24 where we read, "This is the disciple who bears witness of these things, and wrote these things; and *we know* that his witness is true" (italics added). The Gospel had its origin, then, in the oral preaching and teaching of John, the beloved disciple. Friends and disciples probably assisted him in putting it into its present form. A suggestion, recently made, is that the beloved disciple was from Judea and was not one of the twelve. Discussion on authorship will, no doubt, continue.

Where Was John Written?

John shows a remarkably detailed and accurate knowledge of the geography and places of Judea, Samaria, and Galilee. Only a person who had been there or who had access to original tradition could write with such precision. Only John, for example, tells us about such a specific detail as "The Pavement" (John 19:13) where Jesus stood for questioning before Pilate. This was the courtyard of Pilate's Jerusalem headquarters in what was known as the Tower of Antonia, which stood northwest of the temple court. It measured over eight thousand square feet and lay buried under debris after the destruction of Jerusalem in A.D. 70 until archaeological excavations in modern times. Since no other book of the Bible refers to this place, John's knowledge reflects an independent tradition which dates before A.D. 70. The writer also knew about the pool of Bethesda, the presence of which has been confirmed by archaeology. He knew about the mountain where the Samaritans worshiped, namely, Mount Gerizim (4:20), and he knew about the location of Bethany (11:18). At many other points, such as the suggestion of a three-year ministry for Jesus and his explanation of why Jesus dismissed the crowd on the occasion of the feeding of the five thousand (6:15), John's Gospel adds important details to what we are told in Matthew, Mark, and Luke.

John's information supplements the facts given by the other Gospels about the places and events which relate to the life of our Lord. Because of the above details, scholars hold that John was written in or near Palestine. Some scholars suggest that it first appeared in Transjordania or in Syria, which are adjacent territories.

There are some indications in the Gospel that it may have been published originally in a somewhat shorter form, which was subsequently expanded. Since there are no sharp differences in style in John, the original author may well be responsible for expanding his own work. Early tradition associates John with the city of Ephesus. In fact, there was a church dedicated to John in Ephesus, and the traditional grave of John the apostle is located there. One suggestion which has been made is that John the apostle moved from the land of Israel to Asia Minor, to the city of Ephesus, and that in this location he expanded his Gospel in order to meet the needs which his new situation demanded. The Gospel was written for Jew and Greek alike. A new environment called for some new emphases in order to reach the felt needs of the new people among whom John found himself.

John Is Different

There are a number of features in John which mark it as different from the first three Gospels, which are often referred to together as "the Synoptic Gospels." The word "synoptic" in this phrase means that these Gospels look at the life and teachings of Jesus from the same general point of view. John does not take a different, opposing viewpoint, but he does have a somewhat unique approach both in content and method. This is why the Gospel of John is often placed in a category by itself in contrast to the first three Gospels.

John supplements the other Gospels to a high degree. Nine-tenths of the material in John is not found in any of the other Gospels. About the only place where John is rather similar to Matthew, Mark, and Luke is in the account of the trial, death, and resurrection of Jesus. Even here there are many distinctive elements. Another incident which John has in common with each of the other Gospels is the account of the feeding of the five thousand (John 6). Most of the rest of John presents information not contained in the others.

John's vocabulary is in many ways remarkable. He uses short but powerful words which are full of meaning. He loves to use the same words over and over again for emphasis. Here are a few of his favorites which have been placed in columns in order to show how the frequency of his use of these words compares with the frequency of their use in the other Gospels.

	John	Matthew	Mark	Luke
believe	98	11	14	9
to know	57	20	13	28
life	35	7	4	5
light	32	7	1	10
love, to love (agape, agapao)	44	9	6	14
to love (phileo)	13	5	1	2
true, truth	46	2	4	4
witness, to witness	47	4	6	5
world	78	8	2	3

On the other hand, there are some words which John seems to use much less often than do the other Gospel writers. One example would be the word "kingdom," which John uses only five times. It is a common word in the Synoptics, for we find it fifty-seven times in Matthew, twenty times in Mark, and forty-six times in Luke. John seems to prefer to use the word "life" or the expression "eternal life" instead of the "kingdom of God." Entering into the kingdom and receiving eternal life mean for him the same thing. John uses a rather limited vocabulary compared with the other Gospels, but in many ways it is the most powerful and moving of all the Gospel accounts. His graphic style, his play-by-play descriptions of encounters with Jesus, his ability to build up to a climax as he relates some incident— all of these contribute to make John a moving and gripping record of the life and teachings of Jesus.

Other distinctive characteristics of John are his practice of referring to the miracles of Jesus as "signs," the absence of the traditional parables of the kingdom which are so common in the other Gospels, and the omission of the Sermon on the Mount and of the Olivet Discourse about the future as found in Matthew 24 and 25. Unique to John are the seven "I am" sayings. These are:

"I am the bread of life" (6:35).
"I am the light of the world" (8:12).
"I am the door" (10:7, 9).
"I am the good shepherd" (10:11, 14).
"I am the resurrection and the life" (11:25).

"I am the way, and the truth, and the life" (14:6).
"I am the true vine" (15:1).

John loves to move from the physical plane to the spiritual. Events are interpreted so that the readers can understand their deeper meaning. When five thousand are fed through the multiplication of the bread (chapter 6), John affirms that Jesus is the bread of life who came down from heaven. When Jesus asks the woman at the well for a drink of water (chapter 4), the reader is reminded that Jesus is the one who gives "living water." When Jesus opens the eyes of a blind man (chapter 9), it is stated that Jesus is the light of the world. He is the One who makes possible the deliverance from spiritual darkness and blindness to spiritual light and vision. John is always concerned to bring out the deeper, spiritual meaning of the life and ministry of Jesus.

The Dead Sea Scrolls and John

The discovery of the Dead Sea Scrolls in the 1940s made quite an impact on New Testament studies and especially on our understanding of the Gospel According to John. It is not that John directly used the Scrolls or that the writers of the Scrolls knew John. The Scrolls were written many decades before John was written. What their discovery meant, however, was that much which was a puzzle in John, and which some scholars thought reflected Greek influence, is now seen to be material which fit well into the Judaism of the first century. A number of expressions which occur in John and seem different from other parts of the New Testament are also found in the literature of the Scrolls. An example of this would be the expression "the Spirit of truth" (14:17; 15:26; 16:13). Others would be the "sons of light" (12:36) and the expression "practices the truth" (3:21). This terminology is also found in the Dead Sea Scrolls. John, of course, gives each expression his own distinctive meaning. As a result of the discovery of the Scrolls, we do not need to go outside of Palestine in order to explain the distinctive expressions found in the Gospel According to John.

Interpretation in John

Very early in the history of the church some church fathers noted that John was concerned with the spiritual meaning of the coming of Jesus into the world. The author was concerned with interpretation, with what this great event really meant in the lives of individuals. As early as the second century, Clement of Alexandria (as quoted by the church historian Eusebius) wrote about this Gospel: "Last of all, John perceiving that the external facts had been made plain in the gospel, being urged by his friends and inspired by the Spirit, composed a spiritual gospel."[1] Leon Morris points out that in adding this interpretative element, the author of this Gospel did not change the basic facts. Dr. Morris puts it well when he says, "He did not have to distort his facts to accomplish his doctrinal aims. He was able to take what actually happened and speak of it in such a way as to bring out its deeper meaning. John was not trying to impose a pattern on the history, but to draw attention to the pattern that emerges from the history."[2]

When we speak about "interpretation," we do not refer to something which is fiction. All events need interpretation. Our understanding of Jesus has been most significantly increased by what John has written. The word "interpretation" does not imply error of any kind. It simply refers to the fact that the author is concerned to guide his readers into the fullest possible understanding of the implications of the events which have been recorded about Jesus. What did all of this mean? Why is the coming of Jesus important? What does it have to do with the meaning, goal, and purpose of your life and mine? John would tell us that it has everything to do with the life of every person who comes into this world.

Outline for the Gospel

The Gospel According to John divides itself into four parts. We can outline it as follows:

1. The Prologue (1:1-18)
2. The Book of Signs (1:19–12:50)
3. The Book of Glory (13:1–20:31)
4. The Epilogue (21:1-25)[3]

In the so-called "Book of Signs" we find the miracles of Jesus and also many testimonies concerning who he is. This section focuses primarily on answering the questions raised about who Jesus is. In this part of the Gospel, Jesus is presented as manifesting his glory to the world. When we come to John 13:1–20:31, however, we see Jesus speaking privately with his disciples and then finally facing death on the cross in order to complete his work on earth. This section climaxes with the resurrection of Jesus from the dead. In this division of the Gospel, Jesus is presented as manifesting his glory to believers, to those who have become his disciples.

There is a spiral movement throughout John. Certain themes receive repeated emphasis with slight variations. All of this is part of the careful plan of the writer to present clearly his message which centers in Jesus as the manifestation of the Father and as the Savior who brings eternal life to all persons who will put their trust in him and become his disciples.

2

The Word of Life

The Prologue (1:1-18)

The Gospel According to John opens with a poetic prologue which identifies Jesus as the Word (1:1-18). Concerning the Word three things are said:

1. The Word was with God and the Word was God (1:1-2).
2. All things that have been created were made through the Word (1:3-10).
3. The Word took human form, lived on this earth, and revealed God to humankind (1:11-18).

In the Old Testament the word of God is associated with at least three activities of God, namely, creation, revelation, and redemption. In the act of creation God spoke his command, and by that spoken word the creative act took place. In Genesis we read, "Then God said, 'Let there be light'; and there was light" (Genesis 1:3). Again it is stated, "By the word of the Lord the heavens were made, and by the breath of His mouth all their host" (Psalm 33:6). The opening words of the Gospel According to John appear to be deliberately modeled after the opening words of Genesis. Both books commence with the words, "In the beginning," and both then refer to the creation of the world. God's word refers to more than speech. It is God in action. The second concept which in the Old Testament is associated with the word of God is that of revelation. Again and again we read statements like the following: "Hear this word that the LORD has spoken . . ." (Amos 3:1). "Now the word of the LORD came to me saying . . ." (Jeremiah 1:4). Through chosen men and women God made his will known to Israel and through Israel to the world. He revealed himself through his word. The prophet Amos spoke of this in the following passage:

> Surely the Lord God does nothing
> Unless He reveals His secret counsel
> To His servants the prophets.
> A lion has roared! Who will not fear?
> The Lord God has spoken! Who can but prophesy?
> Amos 3:7-8

The third idea closely tied to the word of God in the Old Testament is that of redemption. The word of God delivers men and women from bondage and affliction. The psalmist rejoices in this truth with these words:

> Then they cried out to the Lord in their trouble;
> He saved them out of their distresses.
> He sent His word and healed them,
> And delivered them from their destructions.
> Psalm 107:19-20

The word brought men and women salvation and health. It delivered them from darkness and gloom. It set them free from the bonds which held them fast (107:14). God did all of this because of his loving-kindness (107:21).

These three concepts of creation, revelation, and redemption which in the Old Testament are associated with the word of God are all affirmed by John about Jesus. Regarding the Word which became flesh (John 1:14) he says, "All things came into being through Him" (1:3a). Here the Word is associated with creation. Next he speaks about revelation: "And the Word became flesh, and dwelt among us, and we beheld His glory, glory as of the only begotten from the Father, full of grace and truth" (1:14). Jesus has revealed the Father to us. Revelation is more than facts about God or doctrines to believe. It also makes possible fellowship between God and us. Thirdly, John speaks about redemption. Regarding the Word he says, "But as many as received Him, to them He gave the right to become children of God, even to those who believe in His name" (1:12). He is "the Lamb of God who takes away the sin of the world" (1:29). Creation, revelation, and redemption are all associated with Jesus Christ as the Word.

The prologue is not so much an introduction to the Gospel According to John as it is a summary of its thought and message. It may well have been written last, in the same manner as writers will write the prefaces to their books after they have completed the rest of their work. In the simple but deep words of his opening sentences John gives us the heart of the Good News of God's love for the world which he has demonstrated by sending his only Son to live among us. The invisible God has made himself visible. The unknown God that Greek philosophers sought after has made himself known.

A widely accepted suggestion is that the opening words of the Gospel According to John may at one time actually have been part of an early Christian hymn sung to the praise and honor of Jesus. It may be that Pliny, an early Latin writer of the second century, had such a hymn in mind when he wrote to Trajan concerning Christians, ". . . they were in the habit of meeting on a certain fixed day before it was light, when they sang in alternate verses a hymn to Christ, as to a god. . . ."[1]

The Good News is certainly something to sing about. Early Christians loved to sing, as is shown by these passages:

"And after singing a hymn, they went out to the Mount of Olives" (Mark 14:26).

"And do not get drunk with wine, for that is dissipation, but be filled with the Spirit, speaking to one another in psalms and hymns and spiritual songs, singing and making melody with your heart to the Lord; always giving thanks for all things in the name of our Lord Jesus Christ to God, even the Father" (Ephesians 5:18-20).

"Let the word of Christ richly dwell within you, with all wisdom teaching and admonishing one another with psalms and hymns and spiritual songs, singing with thankfulness in your hearts to God" (Colossians 3:16).

Singing Christians expressed in joy the happy news that light had shone in darkness, that the Savior of the world had come, and that all could now walk in the light which Jesus provides. The message of the Gospel According to John is ultimately the proclamation that Jesus is the One who is the light for living.

The Word (Logos)

The special way in which John speaks of "the Word" is close to the manner in which Proverbs refers to "wisdom." Speaking of wisdom, the writer says,

"The Lord possessed me at the beginning of His way,
Before His works of old.
From everlasting I was established,
From the beginning, from the earliest times of the earth.
When there were no depths I was brought forth,
When there were no springs abounding with water.
Before the mountains were settled,
Before the hills I was brought forth;
While He had not yet made the earth and the fields,
Nor the first dust of the world.
When He established the heavens, I was there,
When He inscribed a circle on the face of the deep,
When He made firm the skies above,
When the springs of the deep became fixed,
When He set for the sea its boundary,
So that the water should not transgress His command,
When He marked out the foundations of the earth;
Then I was beside Him, as a master workman;
And I was daily His delight,
Rejoicing always before Him,
Rejoicing in the world, His earth,
And having my delight in the sons of men."
Proverbs 8:22-31

In this passage wisdom is treated as if it were a person. John goes further than this in his Gospel. The Word *is* a Person. The Word became flesh (John 1:14). The Word became incarnate in Jesus of Nazareth.

The term "Word" *(Logos)* was not one which John created. It was used earlier both in Greek and Hebrew literature. It was used by certain Greek philosophers known as Stoics to mean an active principle in the universe which guides human history. A Jewish philosopher by the name of Philo (d. A.D. 50) used the term to build a bridge between Greek and Hebrew thought. Probably the reason John used this expression was because his readers had been exposed to the term before. It was current, and it provided a point of contact to gain their interest and attention. John used it with his own meaning, however, and that meaning went far beyond anything that the Stoics, the Old Testament, or Philo had ever taught. He identified the Word with Jesus of Nazareth, with God incarnate (1:1, 14). This affirmation that the Word was personal and was God in human flesh was the unique news which John had to share.

The Light of Men

We are told, "In Him was life; and the life was the light of men" (1:4). "Light" in the Gospel of John refers to the spiritual light which Jesus brought into the world. The world was lost in the darkness of sin and unbelief (8:12; 12:35). Jesus Christ came that we might both receive light and become "sons of light" (12:36). What difference does Jesus, as the light, really make in your life and mine? Let us consider just a few of the ways in which this truth significantly changes things for you and me.

1. *Because Jesus is the light of the world, we can be forgiven.*

When Martin Luther was an Augustinian monk, he was much disturbed by a sense of guilt because of his sins. He tried through severe acts of self-denial and even self-punishment to find peace with God, but to no avail. One day his friend and superior in the order, Father Staupitz, said to him, "Martin, love God." Luther replied, "But I can't love him; I fear him." Luther began to study the Scriptures, and suddenly the truth dawned upon him: "he shall gain life who is justified through faith" (Romans 1:17*b*, NEB). He finally realized that peace with God did not come through good works, nor through self-denial, nor through human goodness, but that it came as an unearned and unmerited gift from God. It was the discovery of that truth which changed his life forever. Later he was to write, "For who is able to express what a thing it is, when a man is assured in his heart that God neither is, nor will be angry with him, but will be for ever a merciful and a loving Father unto him, for Christ's sake?"[2] He had discovered the meaning of forgiveness. Faith gave him, as a gift, what he could not earn by good works. As the German theologian Helmut Thielicke has said, "Faith means to receive unspeakable wealth in empty hands."[3]

We don't talk much about sin in our generation. Karl Menninger has spoken of this in his book *Whatever Became of Sin?* He points out that sin is still very much around, but we just call it by different names. We call it crime if it is a serious antisocial act; other actions we may simply refer to as examples of "permissiveness." Changing the name does not alter the fact that there is such a thing as sin. Sin is defined as "transgression of the law of God; disobedience of the divine will . . . failure to realize in conduct and character the moral ideal, at least as fully as possible under existing circumstances; [and finally,] failure to do as one ought towards one's fellow man" (Webster).

By whatever name we call it, we see the lives of men and women burdened because they are not walking in fellowship with God, their Creator and Redeemer. The good news of the gospel is that in Jesus Christ we can indeed be forgiven and cleansed. John put it clearly when he wrote, "Behold, the Lamb of God who takes away the sin of the world!" (1:29).

2. Because Jesus is the light of the world, we can face the future with confidence.

Many fear the future more than they do the past. It is often not a sense of guilt which troubles our generation as much as a sense of meaninglessness. They ask: "What is life all about? Does it have any real meaning? Why am I here? What am I supposed to do?" Jesus gives life meaning. Jesus came as a leader who knows the way to an abundant life with purpose and meaning, for he is the Way. "I am the way, and the truth, and the life; no one comes to the Father, but through Me" (14:6). Following this kind of leader, who is the Truth as well as the Way, leads us to the abundant life God intends for us. Faith is not only faith *in* God, but it is also faith *against* all the appearance of meaninglessness around us. When we have become certain of God, then this certainty will remain with us in all those situations we do not understand and cannot understand.

Dr. Thielicke tells the story of once standing at an open grave when he could find no words to "explain" to the bereaved why this loved one had been taken from them. He made no pretense to have "answers," but he turned their thoughts and faith to One who knows and understands even when we do not. He said to them, "I have no answers for this tragic loss. I am too moved with grief to speak. All I can do is to ask that you bow with me and that together we repeat the Lord's Prayer. 'Our Father who art in heaven . . .'"[4] In God life finds meaning, despite the seeming aimlessness of human tragedy and sorrow. Job was given many "answers" by his would-be comforters, but all of their explanations of his affliction only added to his pain. Finally, however, he met God, and said, "But now my eye sees Thee" (Job 42:5*b*). In that person-to-person meeting Job found no answers; yet the meeting was enough. He bowed in reverence and worship. The Presence of the eternal God, our Father, will sometimes be for us our only stay in the midst of tragedy and sorrow, and yet that will be sufficient to carry us through. The following promise can be ours:

> The eternal God is a dwelling place,
> And underneath are the everlasting arms.
> Deuteronomy 33:27*a*

In the popular movie *Star Wars* one person seeks to give reassurance to another by saying, "May the Force be with you." He refers to a mysterious "force" which he hopes will in some way assist his friend in a dangerous undertaking on which he is about to embark. We as believers in Jesus Christ do not find assurance in some impersonal "force" which will assist us when we are in difficulty. God himself through his Spirit is our source of strength and comfort. Jesus said, "I will not leave you as orphans; I will come to you. If anyone loves Me, he will keep My word; and My Father will love him, and We will come to him, and make Our abode with him" (John 14:18, 23).

We can be confident about the future because we know the end of the story even now. When some people read a novel, they like to look ahead to the last chapter in order to find out how everything turns out in the end. The book of Revelation has given us a picture of the consummation of human history. We can rejoice. Jesus wins in the end. He is destined to be proclaimed King of kings and Lord of lords (Revelation 17:14; 19:16). No wonder Revelation bursts forth with a song of praise and rejoicing: "Hallelujah! For the Lord our God, the Almighty, reigns. Let us rejoice and be glad and give the glory to Him" (19:6*b*-7*a*).

In some of our formal worship services an occasional "Hallelujah" or "Praise the Lord" might bring some vitality into the worship. The story is told of a young man who had recently been converted and who on a certain Sunday morning wandered into a large, imposing, downtown church. At one point during the sermon he was moved by what the minister said, and he simply burst forth with a loud "Praise the Lord!" A dignified elder walked over to him and said quietly, "You can't do that here." "Why not?" asked the young visitor. "After all, I've got religion." The elder responded, "That may be, young man, but you didn't get it here!"

Jesus prayed, "Father, I desire that they also, whom Thou hast given Me, be with Me where I am, in order that they may behold My glory, which Thou hast given Me; for Thou didst love Me before the foundation of the world" (John 17:24). Those who are destined by God to share the final hour of victory need not be fearful about the next minute. Our vision of the future gives meaning to the present. Our assurance of the ultimate day of triumph will not allow any present tragedy or disappointment to crush us utterly.

3. *Because Jesus is the light of the world, we can have the strength for daily living.*

"I am the light of the world; he who follows Me shall not walk in the darkness, but shall have the light of life" (8:12). We do not walk through life alone. Jesus is our companion.

When former President Gerald R. Ford on one occasion addressed the graduating class at the commencement of Gordon-Conwell Theological Seminary, he spoke of his own experience in finding strength through his personal faith in Jesus Christ. He said,

> If the experience of the presidency itself led me to a greater reliance upon God, a greater appreciation of my religion, so did some of the critical events of those two and a half years in the White House. I remember particularly well when in September of 1974, just a few weeks after I had taken office, Betty had her bout with cancer. It was during that time that we came to a much deeper understanding of our personal relationship with Jesus Christ. At a time when human weakness and human frailty was such a real part of our lives, we were able to see clearly for the first time what the Apostle Paul meant when he wrote that Christ's strength is made perfect in our weakness. Having been through that experience, we found that we were better able to give comfort and hope to others in their time of pain.[5]

On one occasion Helmut Thielicke addressed a large gathering of German Christians in East Germany. He reminded them of the ever-present power of God with these words: "So we Christians in the East are by no means as unfree as we sometimes think; we become unfree only to the degree that we underestimate the possibilities of God."[6]

In an article entitled "You Can't Quit," Hubert Humphrey said about his illness with cancer, "If you don't overcome self-pity, the game's all over. . . . But I feel, also, that not all of my life is in my own hands. There is a power beyond man—Divine Providence, the will of

God. It is a powerful source of strength if you can get in tune with it."[7]

Because Jesus is the light of the world, we can with confidence put our lives into his redemptive hands. Because he is the light for daily living, we can with assurance put our future into his directive hands. Because the light of Jesus still shines despite the darkness which has sought to put it out, we can surrender all of our fears and all of our weaknesses into his supportive hands. "Let not your heart be troubled; believe in God, believe also in Me" (14:1).

The Word Was God

When John said that the Word was "with God" (1:1), he emphasized the eternal fellowship of the Word with God. The Word was "in God's presence." The relationship was intimate and personal. The next phrase indicated further that the fellowship enjoyed between the Word and God was on the basis of equality. We read, "And the Word was God." The absence of the definite article with "God" in the Greek original does not mean that we should render this "a god," as some have suggested. Sometimes the absence of the article with a noun stresses the "quality" or "nature" of something. If that is the case here, it would mean that the Word partook fully of the quality of deity. Another simpler explanation for the article's absence here is that it was intended to make clear which noun is the subject of the clause. The presence of the definite article with "Word" shows that this word, and not God, is the subject. We must therefore translate it, "And the Word was God." We would be in error to turn it around and say, "And God was the Word." Both of these explanations have merit.

The Word and Creation

The contrasting statements in John 1:3, "All things came into being through Him; and apart from Him nothing came into being that has come into being," is an example of Hebrew poetry. It is called antithetical parallelism. Two statements are made, one positive and the other negative. They are really saying the same thing. This literary device serves to strengthen and reinforce what is being stated. Other examples of this style of writing in John would be 3:16, 36; 6:50.

The affirmation that the Son of God was active in creation is affirmed elsewhere in the New Testament as well. "Yet for us there is but . . . one Lord, Jesus Christ, through whom are all things, and we exist through Him" (1 Corinthians 8:6). Again we read, "For in Him all things were created, both in the heavens and on earth, visible and invisible, whether thrones or dominions or rulers or authorities—all things have been created through Him and for Him" (Colossians 1:16). Once more we find in Hebrews, "Through whom also He made the world" (Hebrews 1:2*b*).

Light Versus Darkness

"And the light shines in the darkness; and the darkness did not comprehend it" (John 1:5). The Greek word translated "comprehend" in this verse can have two different meanings, depending upon the context. It can mean "understand," or it can mean "overcome." It is ambiguous. This may be why the translators of *The New English Bible* chose to use the verb "master," which can also carry both connotations depending upon the context. One can master a subject, and one can also master an opponent. Since light and darkness in John are presented not only in contrast to each other but also in opposition to each other, the translation "overcome" seems best. This view is supported by the renderings found in Weymouth ("has never overpowered it") and Today's English Version ("has never put it out"). While the Gospel According to John was written to share Good News, we are only five verses into the Gospel before the shadow of the cross falls across its pages. The light of God was opposed by the power of darkness. The knowledge element mentioned above is not far in the background, however, for in 1:10 we read, "And the world did not know Him." There was a refusal to "know" him, that is, to recognize and to acknowledge him and to give to him the honor which he deserved as God's messenger in the world.

In the rejection which Jesus received from the world, from his own people, there was foreshadowed his ultimate rejection which led to the cross. Even this final attempt on the part of the power of evil to snuff out the light was unsuccessful. Jesus rose from the dead; and because of his resurrection, the eternal light continues to shine for all humankind. The concept of light being opposed by the darkness of the world is expressed several times in John. See, for other examples, 3:19; 9:4; 12:35, 46. Ultimately the light overcame the darkness. Jesus triumphed. He is Victor. Therefore, John can proclaim, "But as many as received Him, to them He gave the right to become children of God, even to those who believe in His name" (1:12).

Note that John 1:5 says "the light *shines* in the darkness" (italics added). The present tense is used because that light continues to shine even now. John was not thinking only of the historical ministry of Jesus. Through the proclamation of the gospel by Christians, the light of Jesus Christ continues to shine around the globe. We who are believers are those who reflect and share that light with others.

John the Baptist

"There came a man, sent from God, whose name was John" (1:6). John the Baptist did not appear by pure chance upon the historical scene. The apostle John affirms that he was raised up for his task by God himself. He was the one who prepared the way for Messiah's coming (see the promise in Malachi 3:1). We are told that he came "for a witness" (John 1:7). His role was to be a witness, one who told about Jesus and not about himself. We, too, are bearers of this truth. Sometimes we think we are important in ourselves. The story is told in imagination of the feelings of the donkey who bore Jesus into Jerusalem on the day of his so-called triumphal entry. The donkey was plodding along slowly with head down until he suddenly noticed a crowd gathering and then the people beginning to shout and throw branches into the street. He immediately began to lift up his ears and quicken his pace, thinking, "They are glad to see me. They are applauding me." How many persons whose task it is to bring Christ to the world make the same mistake! Our task is not to seek or to expect glory. We are but the persons who bring Jesus to others. Along this same line it is said of John the Baptist, "He was not the light, but came that he might bear witness of the light" (1:8). There appears to be in the Gospel According to John a definite emphasis upon the subordinate role of John the Baptist (see also 1:15, 20, 30; 3:28, 30; 10:41). Perhaps this stress came as a corrective, not to anything that John the Baptist himself did, but to a John the Baptist movement which continued after his martyrdom. That such a group continued to exist is indicated by the presence of certain people who many years later knew only "John's baptism" (Acts 19:1-7). John the Baptist was one who served with humble self-effacement. How difficult a lesson this is for Christian lay persons and ministers to master! We are all so prone to stress the capital "I." Yet it is in dying that we will find life (John 12:24). The prayer traditionally ascribed to Saint Francis of Assisi expresses this truth beautifully.

Lord,
   make me an instrument of Your peace.

Where there is hatred let me sow love;
Where there is injury, pardon;
Where there is doubt, faith;
Where there is despair, hope;
Where there is darkness, light; and
Where there is sadness, joy.
O divine Master,
grant that I may not so much
Seek to be consoled as to console;
To be understood as to understand;
To be loved as to love;
For it is in giving that we receive;
It is in pardoning that we are pardoned; and
It is in dying that we are born to eternal life.

The Word and the World

"There was the true light which, coming into the world, enlightens every man" (1:9). Note that the KJV applies the phrase "coming into the world" to "every man." This does not catch what is being said here. The verse refers to the incarnation. It refers to the Son of God coming into the world. The reason he came into the world was in order that persons might receive light. To say that he "enlightens every man" does not imply that all persons automatically respond to the light. The light is made available to all. Some responded; others did not (12:37). We must "believe" if the benefits of the light are to be ours. Jesus said, "I have come as light into the world, that everyone who believes in Me may not remain in darkness" (12:46).

". . . the world was made through Him, and the world did not know Him" (1:10). John uses the word "world" in a number of different ways in his Gospel. It is used to mean the physical universe which was created by the Word (17:5, 24). It can refer to the world of humanity, that is, to men and women everywhere. When so used, it does not have a negative meaning but is the object of God's love and concern (3:16; 6:33; 12:47). Most characteristic of John, however, is the use of the word for that which actively opposes God and his people (15:18; 17:14, 25). In the verse before us we are told that the world "did not know Him" (1:10). What this means is that the world refused to believe in Jesus. This was apparently a willful ignorance. It was a deliberate refusal to confess that in Jesus, God had made himself known.

The Children of God

John refers to the early Christians as "children of God" (1:12). To be a child of God means that we have experienced a new birth (3:3). This comes about through the work of God's Spirit in our lives (3:5). There is a second possible meaning to the phrase "children of God." The expression "child of . . ." means that we display the characteristics and qualities of whose children we are. If we are children of God, we will desire to do our heavenly Father's will in our lives. John uses this expression only twice in his Gospel. The other place where it is found is in 11:52. It appears to be one of his designations for the church. A person does not become a member of the body of Christ through physical birth, but through a spiritual act of God (1:13).

"The Word became flesh" (1:14)

This refers to the incarnation. Jesus took upon himself our humanity. He fully identified himself with us. He experienced our sorrows and joys, our pains and happiness. At about the time that John was being written, there arose a heresy within the church which denied that Jesus really had a human body. He only "seemed" to have such a body, said a religious group which became known as the Gnostics. (Note: the "G" is silent in pronunciation.) Their philosophical system was called Gnosticism. They denied the full humanity of Jesus. He was divine, but not truly human. This heresy is strongly opposed in Second John, where a firm warning is given against Gnosticism. There we read: "For many deceivers have gone out into the world, *those who do not acknowledge Jesus Christ as coming in the flesh.* This is the deceiver and the antichrist" (2 John, v. 7, italics added).

When we are told that "the Word . . . dwelt among us," John uses a term which means "to pitch one's tent" or "to tabernacle" among humankind. Jesus came, and then he left, but the world was forever changed because of his brief visit. During the three years of his public ministry, he revealed the glory, majesty, and splendor of God. We are told that he was "full of grace and truth." This expression is taken over directly from the Old Testament where we read about God's "lovingkindness and truth" (Exodus 34:6; Psalm 25:10). The Hebrew and Greek terms behind these English translations are synonymous. Through Jesus, God revealed himself to humanity. He revealed his grace (lovingkindness) and his truth (trustworthiness or faithfulness).

Law and Grace

John talks about grace in verse 16. In using the phrase "grace upon grace," John appears to be stressing that there comes to the believers from God and through Jesus Christ an endless stream of grace. Like the widow's flask of oil (see 1 Kings 17:14-16), it never dries up. One gracious gift and blessing from God is followed by another in endless succession. No wonder John is bursting to tell his story! Good news needs to be shared.

John acknowledges that the law was given through Moses but contrasts this with the "grace and truth" which came through Jesus Christ. The superiority of God's revelation in Jesus Christ is a recurring theme in John's Gospel (see also John 6:32). At the time that John wrote, the church and synagogue were in conflict. The church proclaimed that Jesus was the promised Messiah of Israel. The synagogue rejected this claim and held fast to Moses and the Law. John sought consistently to present Jesus as the fulfillment of Israel's hopes.

Verse 18 with its identification of Jesus as the one who is "in the bosom of the Father" returns to the theme with which the prologue began. This phrase stresses the complete communion which existed between Jesus and the Father. He was God's representative upon this earth. He came to make the Father known. The rest of John's Gospel will be devoted to defending this claim and to giving to the readers a fuller understanding of the revelation of God which Jesus Christ in his life, teachings, miracles, death, and resurrection brought to humankind.

Testimonies to Jesus (1:19-51)

There are two major subdivisions in this section of John:

1. The witness of John the Baptist (1:19-34).
2. The witness of others to Jesus (1:35-51).

Many different titles are given to Jesus in this series of testimonies. He is called "the Lamb of God" (1:29), "the Son of God" (1:34), "Rabbi" (1:38), "Messiah" (1:41), "Him of whom Moses in the Law and also the Prophets wrote" (1:45), and "the King of Israel" (1:49). In these confessions of faith John has gathered most of the important titles given to Jesus during his earthly ministry. After the resurrection the most common title given to Jesus became "Lord" (1 Corinthians

8:6; Romans 10:9). John himself uses this title in what is the climactic confession of the Gospel. This is the confession of Thomas following the resurrection of Jesus when he expresses his faith in the words, "My Lord and my God!" (John 20:28).

Behind the proclamation of Jesus as the Lamb of God (1:29) stands the prophecy of Isaiah 52:13–53:12. Early Christians saw in this Old Testament prophecy not only Israel as God's servant (Isaiah 49:3) but also Jesus who suffered for us on the cross. Philip led the Ethiopian eunuch to confess Jesus as Lord through explaining this passage from Isaiah to him (Acts 8:26-40). The early church also associated Jesus with the Passover lamb (Exodus 12:1). Paul writes, "For Christ our Passover also has been sacrificed" (1 Corinthians 5:7b).

In the concluding verse in the first chapter of John, Jesus refers to himself as the Son of man (John 1:51). He says, "Truly, truly, I say to you, you shall see the heavens opened, and the angels of God ascending and descending upon the Son of Man." This verse reflects the language which described Jacob's dream in which a ladder joined heaven and earth (Genesis 28:12). Angels ascended and descended this ladder. The ladder served to connect God with persons and heaven with earth. The full meaning of Jesus' statement about himself is really that he is the true link between God and humanity. He is the Mediator who makes possible access to the Father. (Compare John 14:6; 1 Timothy 2:5.) What Jacob had dreamed about had become a reality in the person of Jesus Christ. Jesus is the spiritual ladder who joins earth to heaven. The rest of the Gospel According to John expands on this theme and is devoted to developing its implications.

3

Life Through Believing

The Importance of Believing

In the Gospel According to John the miracles performed by Jesus are called by a special name. They are called "signs" (John 2:11). Their purpose is to reveal who Jesus is, and they are intended to lead persons to believe in Jesus as the Christ. The miracles reveal Jesus' "glory." Following the turning of the water into wine (2:1-12), John tells us that Jesus' disciples "believed in him." So important is John's stress on believing that one author entitled his study of John *The Gospel of Belief*.[1] Actually John never uses the noun "belief" or "faith," but he uses the verb "to believe" no less than ninety-eight times. This compares with the other Gospels as follows: Matthew, eleven times; Mark, fourteen times; Luke, nine times.

In the Gospel of John, "to believe" means to respond with the whole person, not just the intellect. To believe involves trust, commitment, allegiance, and obedience. John frequently adds as the object after believing the words "in Jesus." Believing is focused on the person of Jesus Christ. The addition of the words "in Jesus" brings a dynamic dimension to the action, a personal quality of commitment. It means to turn one's life over to Jesus and *to become his disciple*. John uses the expression "to believe in" thirty-six times in his Gospel. This phrase occurs three times in First John and only eight times elsewhere in the New Testament. It is not an expression which is used in secular Greek or in the Greek translation of the Old Testament. It seems, therefore, to express in an almost exclusive way John's peculiar message. The concept of personal trust and reliance was for him the heart of the Christian message. Anything less than this was inadequate. He was not interested in mere acceptance of doctrines. On one rare occasion in John he expresses dissatisfaction with some who "believed." The context makes it clear that in this special case their response was shallow and lacked the total commitment that Jesus demanded of his followers. We read, ". . . many believed in His name, beholding His signs which He was doing. But Jesus, on His part, was not entrusting Himself to them, for He knew all men . . ." (2:23-25). In this instance the so-called "believing" seems to have rested merely on the signs and not in the person to whom the signs pointed. For example, consider the enthusiasm of the five thousand in John 6 when Jesus gave them bread. They wanted to make him king—but on their terms, not his. They had political interests but had no concern for repentance or the spiritual demands of the kingdom of God.

While "believing" is clearly one of John's favorite words, he uses many other verbs with almost the same meaning. Each one of them expresses in some manner a positive response to the person and claims of Jesus. These other verbs include such terms as the following: "to come," "to follow," "to enter," "to drink," "to eat," "to accept," "to receive," "to love," and "to hear."

Of the ninety-eight times that John uses the verb "to believe," seventy-four of them occur in the first twelve chapters of the book. Twenty-four occur in chapters 13 through 21. This difference comes from the main emphases of the two parts of the Gospel According to John. The first section includes the "signs," and these are intended to bring about a believing response from the readers. Here Jesus reveals his glory to the world. From chapter 13 on, the focus is on those who have already made such a response, namely, the disciples. In this latter part of John the stress is on instruction in the Christian life. Discipleship, which finds its beginning with believing, must, if it is to become mature, move on to growth, obedience, and service.

Believing in Jesus means a recognition that Jesus came into the world as God's messenger (7:16, 17). Believing in Jesus means that we confess that he is the Son of God and that in him God is most perfectly revealed (14:9; 20:28). Believing in Jesus means that we yield our lives to him and become his disciples. Jesus said, "If you love Me, you will keep My commandments" (14:15). The result of believing in Jesus is eternal life (20:30-31).

Water into Wine (2:1-12)

We have noted that in John the miracles are usually called "signs." Their main purpose is not to reveal the compassion of Jesus but to manifest his glory. They point beyond themselves to a greater spiritual truth. The miracles are performed on the physical plane, but they are not left there. They are intended to teach us spiritual truth which leads us to a more dynamic belief in Jesus. John uses them as stepping-stones to higher truth. An excellent illustration of John's special approach to the miracles is his account of the feeding of the five thousand (chapter 6). This is the only miracle which is recorded in all four Gospels. The first three Gospels simply tell the story and do not draw any special spiritual lesson from it. In John's account, however, there is attached to the event a long discourse about Jesus as the bread of life which has come down from heaven. This is for John the main significance of the incident. Meeting the physical needs of people was important to Jesus, and it is also a significant part of the Christian ethic for us, too. For John, however, it has a second meaning as well. The fact that a meal was provided for five thousand people is a symbol of something much greater, namely, that Jesus can meet the spiritual hunger of men and women everywhere. That is the universal and eternal truth which the Gospel writer is anxious to share with all of his readers. Almost every miracle in John is accompanied by this two-level understanding. The miracles move from the physical plane to the spiritual, from the local and temporary to the universal and eternal. The one striking exception is the turning of water into wine. John does not attach to this miracle any direct lesson or explanation. Yet he places it as the first miracle and begins his section on the miracles, or signs, with this incident. There appears to be some justification to the opinion that in this particular miracle John is not departing from the pattern he follows elsewhere. He sees in it a spiritual lesson, and we need to ask ourselves what that lesson might be.

We note at the beginning that when Mary, the mother of Jesus, drew Jesus' attention to the shortage of wine that Jesus replied to her, "My hour has not yet come" (2:4). The implication is that when his "hour" would come, he *would* provide wine. Now in John's Gospel, Jesus' "hour" refers to the hour of the cross. We see this in the following two verses, "The hour has come for the Son of Man to be glorified. Truly, truly, I say to you, unless a grain of wheat falls into the earth and dies, it remains by itself alone; but if it dies, it bears much fruit" (12:23-24).

The glorification of the Son in John refers not to the resurrection but to the crucifixion. This is the moment of the supreme revelation of the love of God for the world. In what sense, then, can we associate the providing of wine with the crucifixion? For the answer to this we need to think of Communion. The wine of the Communion cup signifies the blood of Jesus Christ which he shed for the salvation of the world (1 Corinthians 11:25). When Jesus complied with Mary's wish, he did not at that point go to the cross, but his act of turning water into wine foreshadowed and symbolized why he had come into the world and what he had come to do. We can therefore look upon this miracle as a picture, ahead of time, explaining Jesus' mission in the world. It is therefore a most fitting miracle with which to begin both his ministry and John's account of his life and work.

In Matthew Jesus also uses the symbol of new wine to designate the newness of what he had come to do. He introduced the new covenant which replaced the old. His message was not like that of the scribes and the Pharisees who were always quoting some previous opinion. He taught with authority, and everyone was amazed at his message. When the religious leaders refused to accept him, Jesus used a parable to answer them. He said, "Nor do men put new wine into old wineskins; otherwise the wineskins burst, and the wine pours out, and the wineskins are ruined; but they put new wine into fresh wineskins, and both are preserved" (Matthew 9:17).

There may be an implied comparison in John's account of the miracle with what had existed before Jesus came on the scene. The wine the bridal party had before was not as good as the wine which Jesus made. The steward's judgment, which is voiced at the end of the incident, is included as a kind of climactic statement about the whole incident. He says, "You have kept the good wine until now" (John 2:10). With the coming of Jesus the best has come. In Jesus Christ the law and the prophets find their fulfillment. Wine, therefore, becomes a sign of the coming of the messianic times and the dawning of the new age of grace. It therefore ultimately symbolizes the gift of salvation which Jesus brings into the world. Elsewhere in John, other symbols will be used for this, such as the living water, the bread from heaven, and sight for the blind.

The Cleansing of the Temple (2:13-25)

Just as the turning of water into wine has symbolic significance which points beyond the event itself, so Jesus' act of cleansing the temple symbolizes the whole purpose of his ministry. The temple was the place where God was worshiped. It was here that God had promised to meet the people of Israel, to accept their sacrifices, and to forgive their sins. In the statements made by Jesus after he cleansed the temple we can see that a new day has dawned. Jesus began to talk about a new temple. The temple to which he referred was to be destroyed and raised up again in three days (2:19-22). He was speaking not of the physical temple in Jerusalem but of his own body which would die and then be raised to new life. The new approach to God would be through this new temple, namely, through Jesus Christ himself. We do not worship God through the temple at Jerusalem. We worship him through his Spirit, without restrictions as to place and time. That such a day would come Jesus explicitly stated in his conversation with the woman at the well (4:19-24).

In the two incidents which we have looked at—the turning of water into wine and the cleansing of the temple (with Jesus' prediction about his coming death and resurrection)—we are introduced to two themes which run all through this Gospel. The first theme has to do with Jesus' revelation of his glory (2:11). His whole ministry continued to reveal his glory. Everything he did manifested the Father to persons. The second theme is the theme of conflict. When Jesus cleansed the temple, he demonstrated his strong opposition to the way things were. Jesus was, in turn, opposed by the religious leaders of his day. This conflict continued throughout Jesus' ministry and reached a climax in the cross. Beyond the cross, however, lay the resurrection (2:19-22). With these two incidents, namely, the turning of water into wine and the cleansing of the temple, John foreshadows for his readers what lies ahead in the rest of the narrative.

Jesus and Nicodemus (3:1-21)

Nicodemus, a ruler of the Jews, came to see Jesus. He was presumably a member of the Sanhedrin, or council (11:47), the official Jewish court which was composed of seventy persons—including priests, scribes, and elders—and presided over by the high priest. Because of his official status, some interpreters feel that Jesus' reply to Nicodemus can be viewed as a more or less official encounter between Jesus and Judaism. In Nicodemus Jesus met a person who would stand for the understanding and values represented by the Jewish religion.

The encounter with Nicodemus as recorded in John 3 is only the first of three occasions when John tells us about this Jewish religious leader. In his Gospel John portrays for us Nicodemus's pilgrimage. It falls into three parts, namely,

1. Nicodemus the diligent inquirer (3:1-21),
2. Nicodemus the bold defender (7:50-52),
3. Nicodemus the fearless disciple (19:39-40).

Nicodemus came to the one who could give him the answer he needed for the problem which troubled him. We are not told why he came at night. Did he wish to speak to Jesus alone because Jesus was always surrounded by crowds during the day? Did he come at night because he did not wish his reputation to be called into question by his fellow leaders in Judaism? Was Jesus already a person about whom the council had questions? Perhaps the reference to his coming at night means simply that Nicodemus was earnest in seeking answers and would not let the fact that it was evening deter him from obtaining the information he desired.

Early in the conversation Jesus says to Nicodemus, "Truly, truly, I say to you, unless one is born again, he cannot see the kingdom of God" (3:3). In recent years the expression "to be born again" has come into prominence. President Jimmy Carter has referred to himself as a "born-again" Christian. Charles W. Colson, who was involved in Watergate, has written a popular book entitled *Born Again*.[2] Billy Graham has also published a book recently on the subject, *How to Be Born Again*.[3] What really is meant by this expression?

It is only in John 3:3, 7 that this expression occurs in exactly this form in the New Testament. The Greek has two words here. They are the word for "born" *(gennao)* plus the word *anothen* which can mean either "again" or "from above." Nicodemus took the first meaning, and this led to the question he asked, "How can a man be born when he is old? He cannot enter a second time into his mother's womb and be born, can he?" (3:4). Jesus, however, was not talking about another birth of the same kind or quality as the first birth. It is qualitatively different. When Jesus said (see verse 5) that a person needs to be born "of the Spirit," we see what is intended. It is a spiritual rather than a physical birth that he had in mind. In fact, the word *anothen* occurs elsewhere in the Gospel According to John (3:31; 19:11, 23), and in each of these cases the context demands that we translate it as "from above." To be born *anothen* means to be "born of or from God" (1:13; compare 1 John 2:29; 3:9; 4:7). In John 3:31 we read, "He who comes from above [*anothen*] is above all." In 19:11 Jesus talks about power which is given "from above" *(anothen),* and in 19:23 we are told that Jesus' tunic was woven without seam "from top [*anothen*] to bottom" (RSV). The only other place where the phrase "to be born again" occurs is in 1 Peter 1:23. There we have a compound word, *anagennao (gennao* plus *ana,* "again"). While the expression "to be born again" is therefore rare in the New Testament, the idea it represents is by no means unusual. The whole concept of the new covenant suggests the idea of a new creation, a new beginning with the coming of Jesus into the world. With his coming the new age has dawned, and we who follow him become members and partakers of that new age. As the apostle Paul wrote, "Therefore if any man is in Christ, he is a new creature; the old things passed away; behold, new things have come" (2 Corinthians 5:17).

In the course of the conversation Jesus made a rather interesting statement to Nicodemus. He asked, "Are you the teacher of Israel, and do not understand these things?" (John 3:10). Should Nicodemus have known this from Judaism? What is there in the Old Testament which should have prepared him for what Jesus said? Perhaps one of the most instructive passages is found in Ezekiel. Here the prophet proclaims God's word to the people in the following terms:

> "Then I will sprinkle clean water on you, and you will be clean; I will cleanse you from all your filthiness and from all your idols. Moreover, I will give you a new heart and put a new spirit within you; and I will remove the heart of stone from your flesh and give you a heart of flesh. And I will put My Spirit within you and cause you to walk in My statutes, and you will be careful to observe My ordinances" (Ezekiel 36:25-27).

Note how Ezekiel speaks first of the use of clean water to cleanse. This symbolizes repentance and forgiveness. This is the negative, or preparatory, stage. It speaks of cleansing, of the removal of sin. This is followed by the positive gift of God's Spirit which will be placed within those who have been cleansed. As a result of this two-fold experience, it is promised that God will cause them "to walk in" his statutes and cause them "to be careful to observe" his ordinances. Ezekiel appears to be describing the regenerated, born-again person. Repentance, turning to God, conversion (see Psalm 51:10-13) are ideas that are very much at home in the Old Testament. What was partially realized in the Old Testament and what was predicted concerning the messianic age found their fulfillment in Jesus Christ. The hope of Israel had become a reality at last. Nicodemus must have wondered whether indeed the promises were about to be fulfilled. Perhaps that is why he came to Jesus to find out for himself. From what John tells us, Nicodemus took very seriously what Jesus said to him that night, and in a short time he was willing first to defend Jesus before the council (John 7:50-52) and then, finally, boldly to identify himself with the nucleus of disciples who had professed faith in Jesus. At considerable cost he shared with them in the preparation of the body of Jesus for burial (19:39-40).

In Moslem countries the practice of ritual washing is still practiced. For example, outside the El-Aqsa mosque in Jerusalem and outside the Omayyad mosque in Damascus, I have seen Moslem men stop at a large fountain with several spigots, and at one of these turn on the water and wash their face, hands, and feet before entering the mosque to pray. The water does not in itself cleanse spiritually, but it symbolizes repentance and confession of sin. There is an interesting passage in the *Manual of Discipline* in the Dead Sea Scrolls which stresses the fact that a ritual washing just by itself accomplishes nothing if not accompanied by an inner change of heart. It reads in part as follows:

> Anyone who refuses to enter the (ideal) society of God and persists in walking in the stubbornness of his heart shall not be admitted to this community of God's truth. . . . He cannot be cleared by mere ceremonies of atonement, nor cleansed by any waters of ablution. . . . For it is only through the spiritual apprehension of God's truth that man's ways can be properly directed. . . . Only by a spirit of uprightness and humility can his sin be atoned. . . . Only thus can it really be sanctified by waters of purification.[4]

Interpreters differ regarding how the phrase "born of water" in John 3:5 should be understood. Some take it to be parallel to "born of the flesh" in John 3:6. It would then mean the physical birth of an individual. The placing of water and spirit together in Ezekiel, however, suggests that the symbol of water in this verse may well carry the idea of cleansing rather than physical birth. As William Barclay puts it, "Water and the Spirit stand for the cleansing and the strengthening power of Christ, which wipes out the past and which gives us victory in the future."[5] The same suggestion is given by Merrill C. Tenney who writes, "'Water' would recall to the inquirer the ministry of John the Baptist, whose preaching of repentance and of baptism would be fresh in his mind."[6]

There is a definite structure in Nicodemus's conversation with Jesus. It has three parts. Nicodemus makes three statements (verses 2, 4, and 9), and to each of these Jesus gives a reply, each one progressively longer and more complete. It is clear that in reporting the conversation, John intends that what Jesus says to Nicodemus be taken by the readers as words which Jesus also addresses to them. Not only Nicodemus needs to be born again, but each reader of the Gospel does also. Interpreters differ as to where in the narrative Jesus ceases to talk with Nicodemus and where John the writer himself takes up the story in his account of the teachings of Jesus. Some would end the conversation at the close of verse 12, some at the close of verse 15, and still others would carry the conversation through to verse 21. To such a high degree do the style of Jesus' discourses and the style of John's narrative resemble each other that no clear distinction can be made between them on the basis of individual differences.

The Gospel in Miniature (3:16)

It may be said of John 3:16 that in it the full breadth of the gospel is expressed in miniature. The love of God is from eternity to eternity; yet it was at the cross that God demonstrated his love most clearly. The annual rings made on a giant sequoia tree exist throughout the full length of its long trunk. We can see and count them, however, only where the saw has made its cut, for then all the rings are exposed to us. We might say that it was at Calvary that "the cut" was made. It was here that God supremely bared his heart for sinful humanity. As Paul wrote, "But God demonstrates His own love toward us, in that while we were yet sinners, Christ died for us" (Romans 5:8). Such love leads us to join with the hymn writer in saying:

> O Love that wilt not let me go,
> I rest my weary soul in Thee;
> I give Thee back the life I owe,

> That in Thine ocean depths its flow
> May richer, fuller be.[7]

There is in the Gospel According to John a concern both for the world and for the community of faith. In John 3:16 God's love for the world is stressed. In John 13:1b we are reminded of the special concern which Jesus had for his disciples. There we read concerning Jesus, "Having loved His own who were in the world, He loved them to the end." In the upper room discourse the disciples are commanded to love one another (13:34; 15:12, 17). When this Gospel stresses the need for love within the fellowship of faith, the earlier wider concern is not lost from sight. Both messages are important, even as the church today needs to be concerned both for evangelism and for the edification, or building up, of believers. The concern which Jesus had for the world was passed on to his disciples. In John, Jesus commissions his disciples for the task before them with these words: "As the Father has sent Me, I also send you" (20:21).

Once, while on a visit to Boston, I came to the place where D. L. Moody had been a clerk in a store. On a bronze plaque affixed to the wall of a modern building there was this beautiful tribute to the beloved evangelist:

> In a shoe store located on this site there
> was converted to God, D. L. Moody, servant
> of God and lover of men.

D. L. Moody allowed the love of God to become incarnated in his own life, and in that spirit he preached the gospel to his generation.

The Witness of John the Baptist (3:22-30)

In this section John once again bears witness to Jesus. He closes it with the beautiful words, "He must increase, but I must decrease" (3:30). John was a man sent from God (1:6). His life was marked (1) by poverty, living a life of self-denial in the desert; (2) by honesty, fiercely proclaiming the message God had given him to share, and yet willing to express the doubts he sometimes felt (Luke 7:19); and (3) by humility, as expressed in the above passage from John 3. By his ministry, message, and ultimate martyrdom, John bore witness not to himself but to Jesus. Just as John the Baptist pointed not at himself but at Jesus, so we who are Christians are called upon to point our generation to Jesus and not to ourselves. Jesus alone is the Savior of humankind.

"He who comes from above" (3:31-36)

These verses may either be the continuation of John the Baptist's witness or they may be the completion of the earlier discourse which ended at verse 21. In these verses we are told that Jesus is the one who utters the words of God, that he gives the Spirit without measure, and that those who believe on him have eternal life (John 3:34-36). Note that John uses the present tense when he makes this final statement. John uses "life" and "eternal life" as synonyms for salvation. He is not content to think of eternal life as something which believers will inherit some day. As far as he is concerned, it is a present reality, and it becomes the believers' possession when they believe (3:36). At that moment they pass from death to life (5:24). This does not mean that the future aspect is overlooked by John. John speaks of that also (12:25). However, emphasizing the present experience of eternal life is John's distinct contribution. Life for him is centered in fellowship with God (17:3). The life of the age to come has already invaded this world, and we have a foretaste of that which one day will be realized in fullness.

"Beloved, now we are children of God, and it has not appeared as yet what we shall be. We know that, when He appears, we shall be like Him, because we shall see Him just as He is" (1 John 3:2).

From Death to Life

Helmut Thielicke tells the story of cycling into a small German town when he was a young boy. He was tired and hungry. He came to a shop in which there was a large picture of some delicious-looking rolls in the window. He rushed in and said to the woman in the shop, "Please sell me two rolls." The woman looked at him and said, "Why do you ask me for rolls? We don't have any rolls for sale." "But," protested Thielicke, "you advertise them in the window." The woman replied, "Oh, but, son, we are not advertising rolls for sale *here*. We are sign painters, not bakers!" Thielicke raises the question about contemporary Christians and the church in general—are we involved in painting signs or in providing bread? Do we only talk about love, compassion, concern, Good News, and so on? Or do we have bread to give? Has Jesus Christ truly become incarnate in our lives? Does he live within us? Are we channels of living water to our friends? Jesus said, "He who believes in Me . . . 'From his innermost being shall flow rivers of living water'" (John 7:38). In the story recorded in John 4 Jesus took time to minister when he could quite justifiably have just rested a little while from his long journey. Are there fields of opportunity which surround each one of us which we have not noticed? Jesus was sensitive to the hurts of an obscure, and for us unnamed, Samaritan villager. Ministry to others was something that Jesus put ahead of self-concern.

The Savior of the World

John's Gospel stresses that Jesus came in order that he might be the Savior of the world (4:42). John's Gospel has a cosmic or worldwide perspective. In chapter 3 we saw Jesus ministering to a ruler of the Jews. In chapter 4 he deliberately engages in ministry among the Samaritans. No provincialism or narrow nationalism can be seen in John. He takes very seriously the Good News as expressed in the previous chapter when he said, "God so loved *the world*, that He gave His only begotten Son . . ." (3:16, italics added). Jesus opened the eyes of his disciples to the wider opportunities around them when he said to them, "Do you not say, 'There are yet four months, and then comes the harvest'? Behold, I say to you, lift up your eyes, and look on the fields, that they are white for harvest" (4:35). Jesus' attitude toward the Samaritans was a radical break from the way in which his contemporaries regarded them.

There is a stress on social and evangelistic concern in the manner in which Jesus related to the woman at the well. She was a Samaritan, and her background with its mixed religion made her one who was not regarded as religiously pure by the Jews. In addition to this, the story indicates that she was not living a moral life according to the regulations of the law of Moses. Nonetheless, for Jesus she was a person in need. He engaged her in conversation in order that he might genuinely and freely offer to her the "living water" which he had come to the earth to give. Jesus allowed none of the natural religious and social barriers to keep him from ministering to this woman. In what Jesus did for her we can see a lesson both for the disciples and for ourselves. The love and concern of our heavenly Father reaches down to the lowliest, neediest, and weakest of humanity. No one lies outside the circle of his compassion. How we need to learn this lesson over and over again as we consider the intended outreach and impact of the gospel for our own generation! Nationality, race, color, poverty, degree of education, sex, and social customs can all be overcome in Jesus Christ. Men and women can find their oneness in Jesus Christ as Lord. The power of the gospel can set us free from the bondage of prejudice and suspicion which keeps us from reaching out to people who are different from us in some external way. The unity we have in Jesus is greater than any differences which may exist between various peoples of the earth. Jesus' compassion for the Samaritans (even before they responded positively to him) should teach us that love and compassion are appropriate whether or not people give a positive response to our evangelistic efforts. We love them because God loves them, not just because they accept the truths we seek to share.

"Living water" (4:10)

Jesus offers the Samaritan woman "living water." This is another way of saying "eternal life." Those who "drink living water" are entering into fellowship with God (17:3). It implies moving from death to life (5:24), from darkness to light (8:12), and from bondage to freedom (8:36). The Gospel of John reminds us that when we find salvation, we are delivered from rebellion against God and are granted something positive in its place, namely, fellowship and new life. Salvation is deliverance *from* sin and judgment and deliverance *to* a new quality of existence. In addition to fellowship with God, there comes a new oneness to life because Jesus Christ is our Lord, and our life's values now center around the values which he taught.

This does not mean that the full fruit of salvation is instantaneous. Growth is a valid and needed part of discipleship. The disciples made their first decision to follow Jesus when he called them one day along the Sea of Galilee. This, however, was only the first step in an exciting new life of adventure and spiritual development. They were constantly faced with new challenges. They did not always pass the test with flying colors. Nor shall we. They continued, however, to grow. When they fell, they soon picked themselves up. Peter's fearful denial of Jesus did not keep him from repenting of his weakness and reaffirming his devotion after the resurrection. His later life of service is evidence of the sincerity of his reaffirmation of loyalty to Jesus (21:15). Salvation is not complete with a once-for-all crisis experience. Our first commitment to Jesus is but the beginning of a life of continuing discipleship.

Samaria

Who were the Samaritans after all? They were a mixture of native Israelites who had been left in the land after the fall of the Northern Kingdom in 722 B.C. and people from Babylonia and Media who had been brought in by the Assyrians (2 Kings 17:24-34). Jews regarded Samaritans as religious heretics and held them in contempt. The

Samaritans were not allowed to help rebuild the temple when the Jews returned from the exile (Ezra 4:1-5). A permanent division developed between the Jews and the Samaritans which was still present in Jesus' day and which remains even in modern times. While Jesus did not deliberately include Gentile or Samaritan villages in his own ministry or in the ministry of his disciples (Matthew 10:5), it is clear that he intended a wider sphere for the proclamation of the gospel (John 4:35-38; Matthew 28:19-20). During his ministry Jesus broke the stereotype commonly held about the Samaritans. The story of the good Samaritan is the best example of this (Luke 10:25-37).

A few hundred Samaritans still remain today in the area of Nablus, under the shadow of Mount Gerizim. Some other Samaritans live in a few other locations in Israel. When some persons and I visited the area, two Samaritan elders showed us the scroll of the five books of Moses which they prize and upon which they profess to base their faith. An Israeli guide told us that the Samaritans fit in well in modern Israel, and he expected that one day they might be fully integrated back into the nation and lose their identity. For the present, however, they remain a distinct group living peacefully within the borders of Israel.

They still offer sacrifice on Mount Gerizim. The Samaritans have five basic beliefs. They are:

1. Belief in God.
2. Moses is the supreme prophet of God.
3. The five books of Moses are the only valid law of God.
4. Mount Gerizim is the chosen place where God is to be worshiped.
5. There will be a final day of judgment when rewards and punishments will be given by God.[1]

The Samaritans share with orthodox Jews the hope for a prophet who will come as Moses predicted (Deuteronomy 18:18). This prophet, they believe, will reveal further truth and will restore true worship to the land.

Jesus and the Woman at the Well

Jesus came to the well at the sixth hour, that is, high noon. It was hot and he was thirsty. He asked for a drink of water from the woman of Samaria who came to the well to draw water.

The well is still there. It is a little over one hundred feet deep and seven feet in diameter. I have tasted the water, and it is cool, clean, and refreshing. The well is not mentioned in the Old Testament, and it is only here in John that we find it referred to in the New. Christian pilgrims who visited the land in the fourth century were the first to mention its being in this area. It is generally accepted that the well at the foot of Mount Gerizim to which present-day pilgrims are taken is the well spoken of here in the Gospel of John.

Jesus came to "Sychar, near the parcel of ground that Jacob gave to his son Joseph" (John 4:5). The village, which is here called Sychar, is to be identified with the Old Testament place called Shechem. In the Old Syriac translation of John's Gospel, it is actually called Shechem. Recent excavations at Balatah, beside the well, have shown that this identification is correct. In Genesis 48:22 we read that Jacob gave "one mountain slope" or "ridge" (Hebrew: *shechem*) to his son Joseph. In Genesis 33:18-19 we are told that Jacob purchased the land from the sons of Hamor, Shechem's father. Later, in Joshua 24:32 it is indicated that Joseph, after his death in Egypt, was buried at Shechem "in the piece of ground which Jacob had bought from the sons of Hamor the father of Shechem for one hundred pieces of money. [This land] became the inheritance of Joseph's sons." With pride the Samaritan woman reminded Jesus that Jacob had given the Samaritans the well with its refreshing water (John 4:12). She was soon to discover that One "greater than Jacob" stood before her.

The Samaritan woman was surprised that Jesus, a Jew, asked for a drink from her, a Samaritan. Why this surprise? The answer lies in Jewish kosher eating laws. The comment "For Jews have no dealings with Samaritans" (4:9) is translated in *The New English Bible* as follows: "Jews and Samaritans, it should be noted, do not use vessels in common." The Samaritans were religiously and ritually impure according to Jewish standards. Jews would not normally put their lips to a cup from which a Samaritan had drunk. We are reminded of the strict observance of these dietary laws when we are told about Peter's vision when he was asked to eat unclean food. He replied in his dream, "By no means, Lord, for I have never eaten anything unholy and unclean" (Acts 10:14).

John is indirectly teaching his readers a basic lesson through this incident. He is teaching them that Jesus has broken down the barriers which separate people from one another. This is why toward the end of the whole story we find two important summary and climactic statements. The first concerns the fact that the mission of Jesus

Christ, and therefore the mission of the disciples and the church, is for the Samaritans, too (John 4:35). The Samaritans are symbolic of all non-Jews. The second expression stresses once again in different terms the universality of Jesus' mission in the world. It is expressed in the words of the Samaritan villagers themselves when they say to the woman, "It is no longer because of what you said that we believe, for we have heard for ourselves and know that this One is indeed the Savior of the world" (4:42).

The woman misunderstood Jesus' offer (4:11, 15), and her misunderstanding became the occasion for a longer discourse by Jesus which expanded on his teachings. Such misunderstandings on the part of people with whom Jesus spoke are characteristic of John's style of reporting conversations between Jesus and others. They serve as opportunities for an expansion of the particular theme under discussion. Other places where Jesus' words are misunderstood and where the narrative follows with a fuller explanation are John 2:20; 3:4; 6:34; 11:24; and 14:5.

When the Samaritan woman said that her ancestors had worshiped on "this mountain" (4:20), she was referring to Mount Gerizim. Next to it stands Mount Ebal. If one stands near the well, one can see both mountains directly in front of him or her. The one on the left, Mount Gerizim, is covered with trees; the one on the right, Mount Ebal, has no trees because of the rocky slopes of the hill. Mount Gerizim was called the mount of blessing and Mount Ebal the mount of cursing (Deuteronomy 27:11-26). The reason for this was that when the Jews entered the land, representatives of the tribes stood on both mountains. Those on Mount Gerizim pronounced the blessings that would come to the people if they obeyed God and kept his commandments. Other representatives of the tribes, who stood on Mount Ebal, proclaimed the curses that would come upon them if they disobeyed God.

When the Samaritans were not allowed to share in the rebuilding of the temple, they built their own temple on Mount Gerizim. This Samaritan temple was destroyed in 128 B.C. under the Jewish ruler John Hyrcanus. Samaritans continue to worship on Mount Gerizim even though no temple now stands there.

Jesus met the Samaritan woman where she lived—not only where she lived geographically but where she existed emotionally and personally. He was sensitive to her pain and emptiness. He carefully built a bridge between himself and this needy woman. As a result of his care, she found healing both for herself and for others. She, who was probably considered to be a "black sheep" in her community, became a shepherdess. She brought others to Jesus.

The New Beginning

In our study of John thus far we have looked at four separate incidents:

1. the turning of water into wine,
2. the cleansing of the temple,
3. the conversation with Nicodemus, and
4. the conversation with the woman at the well.

At first glance there seems to be nothing which really relates these incidents to one another. Are they simply random events which have been placed side by side, or is there some logical reason why John placed them together? Is there some lesson that runs through all of them which, in a sense, makes them a means for presenting some basic truth? Someone has suggested that in one way or another all these situations point to the "New Beginning" which results from the coming of Jesus Christ into the world. There is a consistent theme of "newness" or of something "better" which has replaced what was formerly present and was inferior. The new replaces the old, as a symbol of the fact that the new covenant takes the place of the old covenant. The "new wine" was "the good wine," that is, it was better than what existed before (John 2:10). We have seen that wine is symbolic of the messianic age. In the person of Jesus something new and better has arrived. Next we see the old temple replaced with the new temple, Jesus' body (2:21). Jesus becomes the new approach to God. We come to God through him rather than through the priesthood and the sacrifices at the temple in Jerusalem. The third incident talks about the "new birth" which is the birth by the Spirit (3:3, 5). The Spirit is God's gift for the new age. Finally, we are told about a "new worship" which is to be in spirit and truth (4:23-24). The restrictions of geography have been removed. By these four separate incidents John really tells his readers that the new age has dawned with the coming of Jesus into the world. The words of the woman at the well carry a meaning greater than she intended when she said to Jesus, "You are not greater than our father Jacob, are You, who gave us the well, and drank of it himself, and his sons, and his cattle?" (4:12). The reader recognizes that this question highlights the point of the whole narrative. The answer to the question is, "Yes, a greater person than Jacob has come." Compare a similar question in chapter 8, "Surely You are not greater than our father Abraham, who died?" (8:53*a*). Again, the answer is, "Yes, the Savior himself has come."

The Life-giving Word (4:46–5:47)

In this section we have two narratives and a discourse. We read first of the healing of the nobleman's son (4:46-54), then the healing of the paralytic at Bethesda (5:1-18); and finally, there is a discourse on the subject of the authority by which Jesus performs his ministry (5:19-47). Jesus needed only to speak the word and healing followed. He said to the official, "Go your way; your son lives" (4:50). From that hour the son began to get better. In the second incident Jesus simply spoke the word to the paralytic, "Arise . . . and walk" (5:8), and he became well. These two miracles are "signs" (4:54) which point to a deeper truth, namely, that it is in the power of Jesus to give *life* to whomever he wishes (5:21). This is the theme of the accompanying discourse with the additional observation that the reason Jesus can do this is because he has this authority from the Father (5:19, 26, 30). The two sick individuals were at the point of death. Jesus gave them physical well-being, or life. These healings were "signs" pointing to the greater truth that Jesus is the source of spiritual healing and eternal life.

The Pool of Bethesda (5:2)

The pool of Bethesda is located in an area northeast of the temple. In Jesus' day it consisted of two pools, one somewhat larger than the other. A walkway twenty feet wide separated the two pools. There were rows of columns on the four sides of the pools and also on the dividing walkway. Together these made the five covered walkways which are mentioned in the story (5:2). The location of the pool of Bethesda has been discovered and can be viewed by contemporary visitors to Jerusalem. Pilgrims in the fourth and fifth centuries spoke of two pools in this location, and they mentioned that the water turned ruddy due to an intermittent flow from a spring. Stairways in the corners made possible descent into the pools.

From Death to Life (5:19-30)

In this important section Jesus is said to be the one who gives life. It is interesting to note that there is a two-fold use of the concept of "life." In 5:19-25 Jesus talks about life as a *present* possession. This is something which the believer receives *now*, the moment he or she commits one's life to Jesus as the Christ, the Son of God. Such a person *"has passed* out of death into life" (John 5:24, italics added). The spiritually dead are referred to in John 5:24-25. When they respond to Jesus, they become spiritually alive.

In the following section (5:28-30), the theme moves to the future. Now the physical resurrection of the dead is mentioned. At this point the futuristic aspect of eternal life is presented. "All who are in the tombs shall hear His voice, and shall come forth . . ." (5:28*b*-29). Some will experience "a resurrection of life" but others "a resurrection of judgment." While John stresses the present aspect of eternal life primarily, this passage makes it clear that the future dimension is not overlooked. Both are important truths, which are an integral part of the Good News which John proclaims concerning Jesus Christ.

Witnesses to Jesus (5:30-47)

By what authority did Jesus do what he did? John tells us that God himself witnessed to Jesus and testified to the fact that he had sent him. It is to God that the word "another" refers in the following statement by Jesus, "If I alone bear witness of Myself, My testimony is not true. There is another who bears witness of Me; and I know that the testimony which He bears of Me is true" (5:31-32). How did the Father bear witness? God bore witness through three separate means. These were:

1. through the ministry of John the Baptist (5:33-35),
2. through the works which Jesus performed (5:36), and
3. through the Scriptures (5:37-40).

The theme which is discussed here, namely, by what authority Jesus did his work, is really basic to the entire Gospel According to John. This Gospel was written to demonstrate conclusively that Jesus came to fulfill not his own mission but God's mission on the earth. He was engaged in a *divine* mission, not his own work (17:4). In Jesus' ministry we encounter God at work in the world.

Is God Still at Work in Our Universe?

In our modern technological world we take for granted the so-called "laws" of our universe to such an extent that we have little room for miracle or for faith. A doctor knows that if he gives a certain medicine, he can expect a predictable result. Does this prove the absence of God? To the person of faith can it not prove the opposite, namely, that in the very order and reliability of the universe we see a divine mind, One who has created things the way they are? Careful mathematical planning can determine the proper orbit into which a rocket needs to be sent and at what speed it needs to be maintained in order to produce a planned result. To the eyes of faith the very regularity and dependability of our world are evidence of the handiwork, sovereignty, and reliability of God. God is not only the God of the unusual and the miraculous. A child finds wonder in a flower, a ladybug, a puppy. We adults walk past these wonders and take them all for granted. Instead of asking, "Where is God?" would it not be more appropriate to ask, "Is there really any place in the universe where we can affirm that God is absent?" Just as the laws which govern this universe are consistent, universal, and everywhere present, so God himself is everywhere present in his universe. This is a truth which the psalmist knew centuries ago. He spoke of it when he said:

Where can I go from Thy Spirit?
Or where can I flee from Thy presence?
If I ascend to heaven, Thou art there;
If I make my bed in Sheol, behold, Thou art there.
If I take the wings of the dawn,
If I dwell in the remotest part of the sea,
Even there Thy hand will lead me,
And Thy right hand will lay hold of me.

Psalm 139:7-10

5

Jesus, the Source of Life

In the next three chapters of John the author uses three different images to symbolize the truth that Jesus is the source of life, namely, (1) Jesus as the bread of life (chapter 6), (2) Jesus as the water of life (chapter 7), and (3) Jesus as the light of life (chapter 8). In each chapter there is included an invitation for persons to respond to Jesus through believing and thereby to receive eternal life. In this section of John we find people voicing strong opposition to Jesus. While some persons become his disciples, others become angry and hostile. They question Jesus' authority and his right to make the claims which he does. They ask, "By what authority do you do these things?" The consistent answer given by Jesus is that he is doing only what his Father has commanded him to do. His authority is not his own but comes from God. This his opponents refuse to believe. The heated discussion often centers on this question of authority, which was also an issue in chapter 5. We shall now look at each of these chapters in turn.

Outline of Chapter 6

This chapter divides itself into three parts:

1. The Feeding of the Five Thousand (6:1-21),

2. The Discourse on the Bread of Life (6:22-59),
3. The Response of the Disciples (6:60-71).

The Feeding of the Five Thousand (6:1-21)

This miracle is the only one recorded in all four Gospels. John's account is unique in that he attaches to the story the discourse concerning Jesus as the bread of life. He also indicates that the response to this discourse is varied. Some of those who had followed Jesus up to this point now withdrew, offended by his teachings (6:60-67). Others, however, including Peter as spokesperson, reaffirmed their loyalty to Jesus (6:68-69).

Just south of Capernaum there is a small inlet in the Sea of Galilee at a place called Tabgha. Here there is a small church built upon the foundation of a fifth-century church which was constructed as a memorial to the occasion when Jesus fed the five thousand. The name "Tabgha" is an Arabic distortion of the Greek name "Heptapegon," meaning "Seven Springs." The church built here is called the Church of the Multiplication of the Loaves and Fish. At the front of the church there is a tile mosaic on which are representations of a small basket of loaves and on either side of the basket two fish. A Greek inscription indicates that the mosaic dates from the sixth century. There is also in the church a beautiful mosaic floor which dates back to the fifth century. This is one of the finest mosaics in Israel and is decorated with various birds and plants that are commonly associated with Egypt. The present church is erected over these mosaics. Tradition has located the scene of Jesus' multiplication of the bread at this place. The sloping hills surrounding the church are green and are covered with grass, as mentioned in John's account (6:10).

The people were hungry. The disciples had no food to feed them nor money to buy enough bread for such a large group. Andrew brought five barley loaves (typical of the food eaten by the poor) and two fish which a young lad had made available. Jesus took the loaves, gave thanks, and distributed the loaves and the fish to the people who were seated on the grass. Everyone was fed, and twelve baskets of fragments remained.

Clearly a miracle had been performed. For John, however, the miracle was only a "sign" of a greater truth. It was proof that Jesus was the bread from heaven who alone can meet the spiritual hunger of humanity (6:35).

"Let's Make Him King!"

The people were amazed at what had taken place. They immediately wanted to make Jesus their leader. They said, "Let's make him king!" (See 6:15.) With these words five thousand men almost began a revolt against the Romans who occupied the land of Israel in Jesus' day. It was an explosive situation. These men were on their way to Jerusalem to celebrate the Passover, Israel's most important festival, the religious holiday which commemorated their liberation from enslavement to Egypt (Exodus 12; John 6:4). We can imagine without too much difficulty how they felt about celebrating independence when they were not free, about thanking God for past deliverance at a time when the yoke of Rome lay heavily upon them. National feelings were strong. They believed God could deliver them again if only he would raise up for them another leader like Moses. Moses had promised that some day a new leader would come. He had said: "The LORD your God will raise up for you a prophet like me from among you, from your countrymen, you shall listen to him" (Deuteronomy 18:15). Moses had continued: "And the LORD said to me, '. . . . I will raise up a prophet from among their countrymen like you, and I will put My words in his mouth, and he shall speak to them all that I command him'" (Deuteronomy 18:17-18). It was this promise that encouraged the hope for freedom. While Joshua took Moses' place in leading Israel after Moses' death, the promise concerning "the prophet" was held to be something which had not yet been fulfilled. "The prophet" was thought of as a forerunner of the Messiah. When he came, he would announce that Israel's new leader was about to appear. Three times in John, and specifically in the passage we are studying, this hope for "the prophet" is mentioned. We find it when leaders came from Jerusalem and asked John the Baptist who he was. They confronted him and said, "Who are you? Are you the Prophet?" (see John 1:19, 21). After Jesus had fed the five thousand with the bread which he had multiplied and which his disciples had distributed, we read: "When therefore the people saw the sign which He had performed, they said, 'This is of a truth the Prophet who is to come into the world'" (6:14). Again in chapter 7, verse 40 we find people saying about Jesus, "This certainly is the Prophet."

As Moses had given manna in the wilderness (6:31), so Jesus gave them bread. We shall see, however, that the real bread which Jesus gives is not made from flour, but is himself. Jesus said, "I am the bread of life; he who comes to Me shall not hunger, and he who believes in Me shall never thirst" (6:35).

The Response of Jesus

How did Jesus react to his sudden popularity? Here five thousand men were prepared to have a coronation. They were ready to put him at the head of their column and sing and dance and shout all the way to Jerusalem. They were ready to cry, "We have found our King!" No doubt, countless thousands of others would have joined the procession. The revolt against Rome, which resulted in the destruction of Jerusalem some forty years later, could well have been launched at this crucial moment. With a very brief but decisive understatement John observes, "Jesus therefore perceiving that they were intending to come and take Him by force, to make Him king, withdrew again to the mountain by Himself alone" (6:15). They wanted to make him king "by force." They were not bowing their knees to him. Rather, they were going to compel him to further their ambitions and aspirations. They were about to make him a pawn to their own strategy, to use him as a tool for their national interests. Jesus would not yield to their promptings. His response was one of disappointment and heartbreak. These people were interested in their stomachs but not in their souls. "Give us bread to eat," they said, "but don't talk to us about the kingdom of God, about discipleship, about self-denial, about obedience to the demands of a holy God. We don't have time for that. We have more practical and pressing problems to worry about. We'll talk about those other matters at a later time."

Jesus quietly withdrew to the mountains alone. By absenting himself from the enthusiastic throng, he effectively put a stop to their political plans. At the beginning of his ministry Jesus had already turned away from the devil's attempt to make him use power in order to achieve God's will on the earth (Luke 4:1-13). Jesus would not be enticed by the external attractiveness of cheering crowds or the glitter of a king's palace. He said, "You shall worship the LORD your God and serve Him only" (Luke 4:8). The Father had set another road before Jesus. It was the path of service, suffering, and self-denial. What these five thousand men wanted to do was the very opposite of God's plan for Jesus, who came as God's servant in the world.

Jesus didn't need this crowd's vote in order to become king. He is a king, but he is king by the will of God and not by the fickle support of a discontented crowd. These people chaffed under Rome. They were enthusiastic about Jesus because they thought he could help them achieve their independence. Provided Jesus met them on *their* terms, they would have been his followers. He gave them bread. They concluded that with his gifts and power he could probably give them everything else they desired. When it turned out later that he didn't fit their preconceived mold for his ministry, their enthusiasm weakened.

Jesus came proclaiming a kingdom. It was a kingdom which centered in righteousness rather than in regal pomp. It called for repentance and faith, not for armies and battles. Instead of lifting the red sword of war, he raised a banner of peace. Rather than rallying one nation to battle against another, he called all persons to a common discipleship under God. A universal brotherhood through repentance and faith was the message and hope he offered. When this became clear, there were those who preferred to say, "We have no king but Caesar" (John 19:15).

Naturalizing Jesus

Is there a danger that we in the twentieth century will also seek to naturalize Jesus, that is, try to make him one of us? Do we put our ambitions and values back upon him so that we claim his support for our "way of life"? It is easy to do that. Some first-year seminary students were asked to write down what they thought Jesus was like. The first young man to share his statement said, "Jesus was an outdoorsman. He was strong and rugged and a natural leader." The student went on to develop his portrait of Jesus. The young fellow who wrote this had been the winner of the cross country run at his college the year before. He was very much interested in sports and active in several of them. His description of Jesus was to some extent a description of his ideal. Most of us tend to do the same thing. We portray Jesus "in our own image." Whatever we value and regard highly, this is what we say Jesus supported.

In the nineteenth century many biographies of Jesus were written. The real problem with them was that all writers stressed what appealed to them. The biographies revealed much more about the ideals and values of the biographers than they did about Jesus of Nazareth. Albert Schweitzer, the famous missionary to Africa, pointed this out very effectively in his book *The Quest of the Historical Jesus*.[1] Liberal theologians of the twentieth century were selecting from the teachings of Jesus that which pleased them and supported their favorite concerns. They ignored much of what Jesus taught. In fact, Schweitzer said that the theologians really missed the heart of Jesus' message, which was the proclamation of the eschatological (that is, future) kingdom of God. Schweitzer maintained that the main thing Jesus taught was that God's kingdom is going to break into this world very shortly and that persons need to repent and prepare themselves for it. He did not just teach, as the theologians had said, great moral and ethical truths of universal significance. So effective was Schweitzer's criticism that for several years people were quite timid about trying to write a so-called "life of Jesus."

We all face the difficulty of being objective. The pacifist finds a pacifist Jesus; the militarist finds support in Jesus' teachings for his position. Each of us tends to stress in the teachings of Jesus that which most supports our present opinion and which is the least disturbing or threatening to it.

Along similar lines, nations sometimes seek to naturalize and nationalize God. Germany had as a motto in World War I *Gott Mit Uns*, "God with us." America puts on its coins "In God We Trust." We all need to remember, however, that no nation can claim God's exclusive blessing and approval. God is God of the whole earth (Psalms 82:8; 83:18). Do not all nations stand under the sovereignty and judgment of God? We in America have a great heritage, but all is not well. Economic and social injustices are widespread. We need to listen again to the teachings of Jesus and to bring our lives under their scrutiny. Jesus remains forever free. We as individuals or as a nation cannot proclaim him king on *our* terms. He will only be king and Lord on his own terms. Jesus said, "Not every one who says to Me, 'Lord, Lord,' will enter the kingdom of heaven; but he who does the will of My Father who is in heaven" (Matthew 7:21).

The Discourse on the Bread of Life (6:22-59)

The central theme of John 6 is the bread of life. The bread multiplied and distributed by Jesus is a symbol of the spiritual bread which he supplies. He is the bread from heaven (John 6:31-32, 38, 41, 50, 51, 58), and this bread stands in contrast to the manna of Moses' day. Therefore, Jesus says, "It is not Moses who has given you the bread out of heaven, but it is My Father who gives you the true bread out of heaven" (6:32). Jesus is not only the means through which God's bread comes to humankind, but also he *is* the bread (6:35). Behind Jesus stands the authority of the Father (6:37-40). Jesus did not come to do his own will but the will of the Father who sent him (6:38).

Jesus met opposition. We are told, "The Jews therefore were grumbling about Him, because He said, 'I am the bread that came down out of heaven'" (6:41). In John the expression "the Jews" is a technical term. It does not refer to the common people, who, of course, were all Jews. So were Jesus and his disciples. The expression "the Jews" refers to the religious leaders of Judaism who had their headquarters in Jerusalem. It refers to the Sadducees who were active in the temple and to the Pharisees who had rules for all of life. Jesus was a threat to the established religious system of his day. These leaders rejected the thought that "he had come down out of heaven." They refused to believe that the teachings of Jesus were inspired by God and had God's authority behind them. His teachings were too threatening, his ideas too radical. In their opinion, he claimed too much authority for himself.

The Hard Saying (6:51-60)

Within the discourse on the bread of life, there is included a statement by Jesus regarding eating the flesh and drinking the blood of the Son of man (6:53-56). This language offended many, and they called it a "difficult statement" (6:60). What really is meant by this response? The central meaning of Jesus' words is that people need personally to respond to Jesus in faith and obedience so that their lives are changed as a result of their experience with him.

The language which we find used here reminds us of the phrasing of the Communion service. Earlier we are told that Jesus "gave thanks" (6:11, 23). Then we meet such familiar terms as "eat," "bread," "give" (6:51), and finally "drink" (6:54). In the feeding of the five thousand Jesus gave them food to eat, but not anything to drink. The addition of the language for "drink" indicates that the Communion terminology has entered into the discussion at this point. The expression "eating the flesh and drinking the blood" are together reminiscent of the "body and blood" represented by the bread and wine of Communion (compare 1 Corinthians 11:23-26).

The Gospel According to John has no mechanical view of salvation through participation in the Lord's Supper. Life does not come to us in that manner. Verse 63 of John 6 helps to make this clear, for it says, "It is the Spirit who gives life; the flesh profits nothing; the words that I have spoken to you are spirit and are life." The Communion is to be participated in by those who have already found Jesus to be the bread of life. John agrees with Paul who taught that external ritual without inner faith is valueless (1 Corinthians 11:27-32). Even as we require bread to eat in order to live, so we need the spiritual bread which God has provided for our inner nourishment. This bread is Jesus the Christ, who came that we might have life "in all its fullness" (John 10:10, NEB). When we compare the wording of John 6:54 with 6:47, we note that "eating the flesh and drinking the blood" are parallel to "believing." These two verses state: *"He who eats My flesh and drinks My blood has eternal life . . ."* (6:54, italics added); *"He who believes has eternal life"* (6:47, italics added). Verse 47 helps to explain verse 54. The "sacramental" language should not lead us to interpret John as holding that salvation comes through the elements of the Communion service. A personal appropriation through believing is the only way salvation comes to us. Communion is important, and participating in it is one way among others in which our spiritual lives are strengthened and built up. No magical or automatic benefit comes from it, however, if we participate with superficial indifference.

By including this discussion in his Gospel, John may have been indirectly repudiating the heresy of Gnosticism which, at the time he wrote, argued that Jesus only seemed to have a human body, but he never really shared our humanity. We recall that 2 John, verse 7, rejected that position. That verse reads, "For many deceivers have gone out into the world, *those who do not acknowledge Jesus Christ as coming in the flesh.* This is the deceiver and the antichrist" (italics added).

The Response of the Disciples (6:60-71)

It is not lack of knowledge, but lack of faith, which explains why some people do not respond to the gospel. Peter expressed well his reason for staying with Jesus. Jesus had asked the Twelve, "You do not want to go away also, do you?" (John 6:67). Peter replied, "Lord, to whom shall we go? You have words of eternal life. And we have believed and have come to know that You are the Holy One of God" (6:68-69). This confession of Peter is closely parallel to Peter's confession as recorded in Matthew 16:13-23; Mark 8:27-33; and Luke 9:18-22.

Personal experience is often the best test of truth. As Jesus said, "If any man is willing to do His will, he shall know of the teaching, whether it is of God, or whether I speak from Myself" (John 7:17). The strongest argument for the truth of the gospel lies in the quality of the lives of those who have been transformed by the risen Lord. Malcolm Muggeridge, the former editor of *Punch* magazine in England, expressed this truth well when he wrote in his book *Jesus, the Man Who Lives:* ". . . in the dismal slums of Calcutta a Mother Teresa and her Missionaries of Charity go about Jesus's work of love with incomparable dedication. . . . What commentary . . . can equal . . . the effect of these dedicated lives?"[2] On another occasion he said about his feelings when the time came for him to say good-bye to Mother Teresa: ". . . I felt as though I were leaving behind me all the beauty and all the joy in the universe. Something of God's universal love has rubbed off on Mother Teresa. . . ."[3] Her life was beautiful in Christian service as she ministered unselfishly in Jesus' name to the sick and dying poor of that great city.

Opposition to Jesus (John 7 and 8)

In John 7 and 8 we have a series of controversial dialogues between Jesus and his opponents. John has gathered together a long list of objections which had been raised against the claim that Jesus was the promised Messiah of Israel. To each of the objections a defense or response is given. We may note these briefly, giving first the objection raised and then the reply.

1. Jesus works in secret (7:4).
   Answer: Jesus also speaks openly (7:26).
2. Jesus leads the people astray (7:12).
   Answer: He is teaching them God's truth (7:16-18).
3. He has never studied (7:15).
   Answer: His teaching is God's teaching, not his own (7:16).
4. He has a demon (7:20; 8:48).
   Answer: He has no demon but is honoring his Father (8:49).
5. No one knows where the Messiah will come from, but we know where Jesus comes from (7:27).
   Answer: Jesus' place of origin is not just Galilee; he has come from God (7:29; 8:14).
6. The Messiah will not come from Galilee (7:41).
   Answer: He came from God (8:14).
7. The authorities and the Pharisees have not believed (7:48).
   Answer: Some did believe (8:30; 12:42). Nicodemus, one of them, speaks in Jesus' defense (7:50-51).

8. Jesus bears witness to himself (8:13).

Answer: The Father also bears witness to Jesus (8:18).

John has brought together here replies to Jewish objections against the messianic claims of Jesus. Presumably John's interest was more than historical. By what he wrote he provides his readers with a defense of the Christian belief that Jesus is Lord, against continuing objections by synagogue representatives.

Jesus, the Water of Life (7:1-52)

The setting for chapters 7 and 8 is the temple in Jerusalem. The occasion is the Feast of Tabernacles (7:2). This is also called the Feast of Booths, or, in Hebrew, Succoth. Being a harvest festival, it falls in October and lasts seven days, plus two days which were added at a later time. The ninth day is called Simhath Torah, meaning, "Joy of the Law." This was an occasion for rejoicing in the gift of the law and involved celebration and dancing with the scrolls. Originally the feast commemorated the wilderness wanderings (Leviticus 23:39-43; Deuteronomy 16:13-15). There were three great feasts in Israel's religious calendar. These were: (1) Passover, which was also known as the Feast of Unleavened Bread, (2) Tabernacles, and (3) the Feast of Weeks. During these three festivals adult males in Israel were expected to make a pilgrimage to Jerusalem to the temple.

On each of the seven mornings of the Feast of Tabernacles a procession of priests from the temple went down to the pool of Siloam. This reservoir, which received its water from the Gihon Spring, was built around 700 B.C. by King Hezekiah. It was the main source of water for the city of Jerusalem. A golden pitcher was filled with water at the Pool of Siloam, and as the procession returned to the temple, a choir sang from Isaiah 12:3 the words,

> Therefore you will joyously draw water
> From the springs of salvation.

They also sang a group of psalms known as the Hallel Psalms (Psalms 113–118). They marched around the altar of burnt sacrifice and sang Psalm 118:25, "O LORD, do save, we beseech Thee." A priest then ascended the altar and poured the water which had been brought into a silver funnel. This water flowed down into the ground as a libation, or offering, to the Lord. This procedure was followed each of the seven mornings of the festival except that on the seventh day they marched around the altar seven times.

In the light of this special use of water as a symbol for salvation in the celebration of the Feast of Tabernacles, the actions and words of Jesus in John 7 take on fresh and exciting meaning. Now we can understand more fully the occasion and real significance of the invitation made by Jesus: "Now on the last day, the great day of the feast, Jesus stood and cried out, saying, 'If any man is thirsty, let him come to Me and drink. He who believes in Me, as the Scripture said, "From his innermost being shall flow rivers of living water"'" (John 7:37-38). Jesus is the true water of life. Jesus turns the symbolism of the ceremony into reality (compare Isaiah 44:3; 55:1). It is clear that John recognized the relationship between the festival and Jesus' offer. In a dramatic way John shows how the proclamation of Jesus was tied to the temple ritual.

Another possible way to translate this passage is to regard these verses as reflecting the parallelism of Hebrew poetry. *The New English Bible* does this, and the translation which then results is as follows: "On the last and greatest day of the festival Jesus stood and cried aloud, 'If anyone is thirsty let him come to me; whoever believes in me, let him drink.' As Scripture says, 'Streams of living water shall flow out from within him'" (John 7:37-38). The last line would then refer to Jesus who is the source of living water to those who believe.

The Woman Caught in Adultery (7:53–8:11)

This incident is omitted in the most ancient and best manuscripts. It appears to have been added later by an unknown scribe. It may, however, be a true incident in the ministry of Jesus and for this reason was repeated by oral tradition and subsequently attached here to John. Some manuscripts include it after John 21:24, and one places it after Luke 21:38. The compassion which Jesus shows for the woman in the story is certainly in keeping with the way Jesus ministered to people.

Jesus, the Light of Life (8:12-59)

This story completes the series of three images of Jesus. We began with Jesus as "the bread of life" (John 6); then we saw Jesus as "the water of life" (John 7); now we see him as "the light of life." Once again we note the theme of life, which runs not only through these three chapters but also throughout the entire Gospel.

It is interesting to note that just as the truth about Jesus as the source of living water was tied to the Feast of Tabernacles, so his proclamation of himself as "the light of the world" is closely related to actual practices carried on at the temple during this festival. On the occasion of the Feast of Tabernacles four huge lamps were lit in the temple court. At the top of these lamps were golden bowls filled with olive oil. When lit, they gave light to the entire temple area and to much of the surrounding city. During each of the seven nights of the festival, there were a torch dance and flute playing, and the Levites who performed the temple service chanted the Psalms of Ascent (120–134).

With this ritual in mind we can understand better why Jesus said, "I am the light of the world; he who follows Me shall not walk in the darkness, but shall have the light of life" (John 8:12). He was claiming that the light of the Lord, symbolized by the candelabra, was fulfilled in himself.

"The Son shall make you free" (8:36)

Each one of us is constantly faced with the challenge of living our lives either in obedience to the Father or in a self-centered rebellion against his will. Only in the Father's house can we find true freedom. The "far country" leads to the bondage of many inner and outer masters, not to true freedom (see Luke 15:13-14). Genuine discipleship means more than an initial decision to believe in Jesus. It calls for steadfastness of faith. We are to abide in his word (8:31). In submitting to the lordship of Jesus over our lives, we find freedom (8:36). The more we become his bondslaves, the more we shall be freed from self and sin and the more we shall experience the "fullness of life" which Jesus came into the world to give (see John 10:10).

Life in Fullness

Jesus Manifests Himself as the Light of Life (9:1-41)

I have a friend who works at the General Electric Space Center in King of Prussia, Pennsylvania. On one occasion when I visited the facility, he showed me a Nimbus weather satellite which was then under construction. It obviously involved very intricate and complicated engineering. Two years were required for its completion. Among the items which interested me particularly were two solar panels attached to the satellite. The purpose of these panels was to obtain energy from the sun. These solar panels were absolutely essential for the proper functioning of the satellite. Without the light from the sun, the energy stored up in the satellite would soon be used up.

There is another light in this world which is equally necessary. This greater light, says John, is Jesus Christ. In words that echo Jesus' statement in the previous chapter (see 8:12), Jesus says, "While I am in the world, I am the light of the world" (9:5). Even as the satellite obtains its energy from the sun, so believers derive their spiritual life from Jesus of Nazareth. He is the mediator who brings the life and light of God to us. Jesus is the light because he reveals the Father who is light. As we read in First John, "God is light, and in Him there is no darkness at all" (1 John 1:5*b*).

The categories of light and darkness to express good and evil appear in the Old Testament and also in the writings we call the Dead Sea Scrolls. One of the sectarian documents included in the Dead Sea Scrolls discovery is called "The War of the Sons of Light and the Sons of Darkness." The phrasing reminds us of Jesus' words to his disciples, "While you have the light, believe in the light, in order that you may become sons of light" (John 12:36). In darkness evil is practiced. We remember the blackout in New York City some time ago, when looting and destruction of property took place. Even as physical light counters evil, so the spiritual light which radiates from Jesus into the world opposes the evil which is so much a part of human existence.

God's light also purifies. It directs our footsteps in the way we should go. As the psalmist put it,

> Thy word is a lamp to my feet,
> And a light to my path.
> Psalm 119:105

To walk in God's light is to walk in obedience to his will. The future city, the new Jerusalem, will be characterized by light. We read, "And the city has no need of the sun or of the moon to shine upon it, for the glory of God has illumined it, and its lamp is the Lamb. . . . (for there shall be no night there) . . ." (Revelation 21:23-25).

In this chapter we read about Jesus' opening the eyes of a man born blind. Such miracles are also recorded in the other Gospels (see, for example, Matthew 11:5; 12:22; Mark 10:52). As is typical of John's practice, however, he attaches to the miracle a discourse which turns the event into a "sign." The miracle points beyond itself to the greater truth that Jesus is the light of the world and that he is the One who can open the eyes of persons who are spiritually blind because of sin. Unbelief and spiritual blindness are regarded as part of the same problem in the Gospels (see Matthew 15:14; 23:16; John 9:39-41).

The Gihon Spring, the Pool of Siloam, and Hezekiah's Tunnel

Jesus anointed the man's eyes and told him to go and wash in the pool of Siloam (John 9:7). This pool still exists in Jerusalem and can be seen by the contemporary visitor to the city. It is a rectangular pool which is about twenty feet by thirty feet in size. The reason such a pool was located within the walls of the city of Jerusalem is because of the foresight of an ancient king in Israel by the name of Hezekiah, who reigned from 715 to 687 B.C. He determined that the water from the Gihon Spring, which lay outside the city walls, needed to be available to the city's inhabitants in case of siege. He therefore gave to engineers and workmen the task of building a tunnel through the rock and under the walls, in order to bring the water within the city proper. It was a difficult engineering task, but it was carried out successfully. When the tunnel was finished, the water flowed, as planned, from the Gihon Spring to the pool of Siloam. Hezekiah then completely blocked and closed any access to the Gihon Spring from outside the city walls. What had prompted his action was the threat of Assyria. The people said, "Why should the kings of Assyria come and find abundant water?" (2 Chronicles 32:4). The story of Hezekiah's accomplishments with regard to the diverting of the water is told in 2 Kings 20:20 and 2 Chronicles 32:3-4, 30.

On one occasion I had the thrilling experience of walking through the tunnel Hezekiah built. Five of us started at the Gihon Spring and waded with water up to our waists until we came out at the open-air pool of Siloam. We found our way through the 1,749-foot tunnel with the aid of candles. The tunnel is in the form of a large S. At one point four of the candles went out because of drafts in the tunnel. We gathered close together and lit them with the one candle which remained burning. We worked our way slowly through the tunnel, which at times was less than six feet high and was only about two feet wide. In 1880, an interesting inscription had been discovered on the wall of the tunnel near its entrance. This inscription, subsequently removed and placed in the Imperial Museum in Istanbul, Turkey, when translated, reads as follows:

> The boring through is completed. Now this is the story of the boring through. While the workmen were still lifting pick to pick, each towards his neighbour, and while three cubits remained to be cut through, each heard the voice of the other who called his neighbour, since there was a crevice in the rock on the right side. And on the day of the boring through the stone-cutters struck, each to meet his fellow, pick to pick; and there flowed the waters to the pool for a thousand and two hundred cubits, and a hundred cubits was the height of the rock above the heads of the stone-cutters. [1]

Two teams of workers worked on the tunnel, beginning from opposite ends. The inscription tells of the meeting of the two teams. For many years the Gihon Spring was the principal source of water for the city of Jerusalem.

Jesus and the Man Born Blind

The story of Jesus' encounter with this blind man is told in such a vivid way that Raymond E. Brown has said of it, "We have here Johannine dramatic skill at its best."[2] We note immediately the contrast between the beginning of the story and its conclusion. When the incident opens, the man we meet is blind; when it closes, he has his sight. On the other hand, the Pharisees, who claim to be spiritual leaders in Israel and who put the healed man through intensive questioning in which they seek to disprove the miracle which took place, are at the end of the story the persons who are declared to be blind, that is, spiritually blind. Their blindness is qualified by the statement that it is caused by their refusal to see, that is, their refusal to acknowledge that in and through Jesus God has performed a miracle. If their blindness were of such a nature that they could do nothing about it, then Jesus says they could not be held accountable. Instead they are willfully blind, while claiming spiritual insight, and for this reason they remain condemned in their blindness (John 9:40-41).

The blind man is presented as moving from one stage of understanding to the next in a stairstep progress. His knowledge deepens with each step. First he calls Jesus, "the man who is called Jesus" (9:11). Next he progresses to affirm that Jesus is "a prophet" (9:17). His third step is to argue that Jesus must be "from God" (9:33). Finally, as he encounters Jesus after the healing, we are told that he said to Jesus, "Lord, I believe," and that he then "worshiped Him" (9:38). It appears that John has deliberately demonstrated this progressive development in the blind man's understanding and faith. The climactic confession at the end is intended, in part at least, as a model of the kind of confession to which John desires that all of his readers may also come. Leading persons to confess that Jesus is "Lord" is the stated purpose of this Gospel (20:30-31).

"Do you believe?" (9:35)

The blind man came to believe because he had gained his sight. There can ultimately be no stronger argument than that of personal experience. The closer our own walk is with the Lord, the more we, too, will grow in faith and Christian maturity. We need always to be dissatisfied with the level of maturity we have already attained. There is constantly new light to be obtained and fresh commitments to be made. When we turn from the light, we will walk in the shadow caused by our unbelief. When we walk in his light, our path grows brighter day by day. The following poem expresses the thought well.

I Heard the Voice of Jesus
I heard the voice of Jesus say,
"I am this dark world's light;
Look unto Me, thy morn shall rise,
And all thy day be bright:"
I look'd to Jesus, and I found
In Him my star, my sun;
And in that light of life I'll walk
Till travelling days are done.[3]

Jesus, the Good Shepherd (10:1-42)

On one occasion while in Jerusalem, I wished to buy a present for a friend who is a minister here in the United States. Not knowing just what to buy, I decided to look through some of the many shops in the old walled city. Going through the Damascus Gate into the old city, I walked by fruit and vegetable stands which sold everything from prickly cactus pears to apricots, bananas, cucumbers, and beans. I passed Arab men, many in long, flowing robes and with Arab headdresses, in conversation sitting at small tables outside coffee shops, some playing chess and smoking Turkish water pipes. I saw many Arab women shopping in long black dresses beautifully embroidered. An Arab vendor stood at the street corner selling coffee from a huge silver container that he had strapped on his back. Now and then a beggar requested alms. These sights, sounds, and smells are all very familiar to anyone who has traveled in the Arab lands of the Middle East.

Donkeys mingled with people as I strolled in the narrow, twisted streets. I walked through the street of the butchers and then came to the street with dry goods and leather shops. Some of these little stores were able to hold only three or four customers at a time. I entered a small shop and looked at the display of the merchandise for sale. There were multicolored candles, native jewelry, mother of pearl jewelry boxes, bags made of camel hide, and copper trays with attractive, carefully hammered geometric designs. Among the olivewood products there were camels with long necks and donkeys with long ears. There were also candle sticks of various sizes. One olivewood carving, which was about six inches tall, especially caught my eye. It was that of a shepherd. Dressed in rough garb, and with a pouch at his side, the shepherd was slightly bent over. On his shoulders he was carrying a lamb. I picked up the carving and admired it. After some good-natured bargaining, I purchased this object. It reminded me both of Jesus' parable of the good shepherd and of Jesus himself as our Shepherd.

Shepherds remain familiar figures among the Arab residents of Israel. Often mixed flocks and herds of sheep and black-haired goats can be seen grazing on the hillsides. On the Jewish communal farms, sheep are kept for milking. The main part of Judea, the central section of modern Israel between Galilee and the Negev, is a high plateau, which lends itself to the raising of sheep and goats. The image of the shepherd is a common one in both the Old and New Testaments. Christian pastors are viewed as shepherds (John 21:15-16; Acts 20:28-29), while Jesus is the chief Shepherd (1 Peter 5:2-4; cf. Hebrews 13:20).

The occasion for Jesus' discourse on the good shepherd was the Feast of the Dedication (John 10:22). This feast is better known in the Jewish community today as Hanukkah. It commemorates an event which is not described in the Bible because it took place between the times of the writings of the Old and New Testaments. It honors the rededication of the Jewish temple in Jerusalem in December, 165 B.C., under the Jewish freedom fighters known as the Maccabees. The temple had been desecrated by Antiochus Epiphanes by his dedicating it to the Greek god Zeus Olympius two years earlier. This ruler controlled Palestine from his headquarters in Syria. Because of the struggle of the Maccabees, the Jews obtained religious freedom first, and finally political freedom in 142 B.C. According to one suggestion, the regular readings in the synagogues on the sabbath nearest the Feast of the Dedication were taken from Ezekiel 34 and were concerned with the theme of the shepherd and the sheep.[4] If this is so, then Jesus' sermon is directly tied in to a Jewish festival, as his sermons were in John 7 and 8.

The Image of the Church

The Gospel According to John reflects a deep interest in the church. John never uses the word "church" as such, but he frequently refers to it indirectly. Actually, the word "church" is not found in Mark or Luke either. The only place the term is used in the Gospels is in Matthew (16:18; 18:17). The two most important symbols for the church which we find in John are the images of the shepherd and the sheep (John 10:1-29) and of the vine and the branches (15:1-7). Other images for the church found in John include "the bride and the bridegroom" (3:29); "the children of God" (1:12); "the people" (11:49-50; 18:14); "his own" (13:1); and the "flock" (10:16).

In the chapter before us Jesus identifies himself as "the good shepherd" (10:11). Many passages in the Old Testament compare God and Israel to the shepherd and the sheep. Jesus is here using Old Testament imagery and applying it to himself and his followers. The fellowship of the Old Testament saints was a reality for the nucleus of disciples around Jesus. In the Old Testament the following passages come to mind to illustrate God as Israel's shepherd:

> The Lord is my shepherd,
> I shall not want.
> > Psalm 23:1

> Oh give ear, Shepherd of Israel,
> Thou who dost lead Joseph like a flock. . . .
> > Psalm 80:1

> Like a shepherd He will tend His flock,
> In His arm He will gather the lambs,
> And carry them in His bosom;
> He will gently lead the nursing ewes.
> > Isaiah 40:11

Two similar passages are found in Psalm 100:3 and Ezekiel 34:1-31. Ezekiel pictures God as the ideal shepherd. Through Ezekiel God says, "'I will feed My flock and I will lead them to rest" (Ezekiel 34:15). God is portrayed in contrast to the faithless shepherds of Israel whom Ezekiel indicts because they plunder the flock. There is a similar indictment in Jesus' portrayal of the spiritual shepherds of his day (John 10:12-13). The theme of the suffering servant of Isaiah 53:7-12 is in John interwoven with the theme of the self-denying shepherd. He gives his life for the sheep (John 10:11).

"One flock, with one shepherd" (10:16)

There is in John a play on words in this expression. In Greek this reads: *mia poimne, heis poimen*. There is only one letter transposed which distinguishes the first noun from the second. By this phrase the unity of the church is being emphasized. It is possible that the expression stresses the unity of the church despite the inclusion of Gentiles. Jesus says earlier, "I have other sheep, which are not of this fold; I must bring them also, and they will hear My voice..." (10:16). Jesus seems to be referring to Gentiles who will respond to him and who will become part of the same flock as the Jewish disciples. The same emphasis upon unity can be found in Ephesians 2:14-22 and 4:1-6. This understanding of the gospel as intended for all people is an emphasis found elsewhere in John (1:12; 3:16; 4:42).

"They follow Me" (10:27)

Sheep follow their shepherd. My father-in-law used to keep sheep on his farm in Indiana. Whenever he came near the fence, they would approach him. When I as a stranger would appear, they would shy away. They were afraid of me and tried to avoid me. This experience reminded me of Jesus' words, "A stranger they simply will not follow, but will flee from him, because they do not know the voice of strangers" (10:5). In some ways sheep are smarter than Christians. We tend all too often to listen to the voice of the tempter instead of keeping our ears open only to the voice of Jesus our Shepherd. As the shepherd goes before the sheep, so Jesus goes before us. If we will but follow him and heed his voice, he will lead us into the fullness of life which he has promised. He will protect us from all spiritual dangers. Jesus said, "I give eternal life to them, and they shall never perish; and no one shall snatch them out of My hand" (10:28). When we do not heed his voice, our ears become dull and insensitive; we wander afar off; we enter areas of spiritual danger; and we lose our sense of peace and security which we can have only when we are in the good Shepherd's presence. We need him to protect us. The sheep have little that they can do to protect themselves. While not entirely defenseless, sheep are certainly one of the animals least able to fight in their own defense.

The Shepherd's Love

Jesus spoke of the shepherd who would leave ninety-nine sheep in order to find one that was lost (Luke 15:3-7). Just as the good shepherd lays down his life in order that the sheep may live, so Jesus laid down his life so that men and women might find "life" through him (John 10:10-11). This life is a *present* possession as well as a *future* hope (3:36; 4:36). This life finds its central meaning in fellowship with God (17:3). It speaks of a new quality of existence so dramatically different from our life apart from God that the former existence can be spoken of as "death" (5:24). John's whole purpose in writing was to urge his readers to receive this new life, which was made possible through the coming of Jesus into the world (20:30-31).

Today's Imagery

For people brought up in the city the illustration of a shepherd and his sheep may leave something to be desired. Perhaps young people today might think instead of a coach and his or her team. A good coach trains, disciplines, and encourages the team. A coach watches over the health of the players. The reason we keep hearing that new records have been set in the Olympics is not just because young people are naturally more athletic today but because they have some of the finest coaching ever available. Christian young people can think of Jesus Christ as their spiritual coach. They are being coached for the greatest game they will ever play, namely, the game of life.

Parents play much the same role as coaches—only it is our privilege and responsibility to give leadership to our children over a much longer period of time and in almost every area of their lives. As long as we can keep the doors of communication between our children and us open, influence can continue to walk back and forth. We who are parents also work under a coach. We get our signals from the Lord. It is our responsibility to bring up our children not simply according to our system of values but in the nurture and admonition of the One who is coach and Lord over all of life.

The Raising of Lazarus (11:1-57)

The main interest in this incident is not Lazarus, but Jesus. We are not told what happened to Lazarus after he was raised from the dead. The key to the whole story is the pronouncement which Jesus made: "I am the resurrection and the life; he who believes in Me shall live even if he dies, and everyone who lives and believes in Me shall never die" (11:25-26). The story of the resurrection of Lazarus was included by John in order to illustrate the deeper spiritual truth that Jesus is the one who raises persons from the state of spiritual death and separation from God. For John the incident, based on fact, was symbolic of Jesus as the resurrection and the life. He recorded the incident as a "sign" in order that the readers may also believe in Jesus.

The setting of the story is Bethany, on the Mount of Olives.

Bethany is a suburb of Jerusalem, across the Kidron Valley and on the eastern slopes of the Mount of Olives. Today the name for Bethany is El 'Azariyeh, which is the Arabic form of Lazarium, the name given to the village by Christians in the fourth century.

We should not equate the raising of Lazarus with the raising of Jesus. Lazarus rose again to *this* life, and there is no indication that he was not mortal, nor that he did not die again at some later date. Jesus rose to newness of life. He was the first fruits of a new creation (1 Corinthians 15:20). As Paul wrote, "Christ, having been raised from the dead, is never to die again; death no longer is master over Him" (Romans 6:9).

Perhaps the reason John stressed that Jesus waited for four days before he came to the grave was in order that everyone might know that there was no question about the fact that Lazarus was definitely dead. There was a popular Jewish belief that the soul of the deceased remained near the body for three days after death and then departed.[5] On the fourth day the soul was supposed to leave. There is no biblical basis for such a belief, but perhaps John was aware of this tradition and wished to remove all doubt about the reality of Lazarus' death.

The council, or Sanhedrin, the ruling body of the Jews, used the raising of Lazarus as the occasion to plot the death of Jesus (John 11:47-48). Caiaphas spoke words which carried a double meaning, the deeper significance of which he apparently did not intend, but John saw his words as a prophecy which the high priest uttered under divine inspiration. He said, ". . . it is expedient for you that one man should die for the people, and that the whole nation should not perish" (11:50). What he meant was that they should get rid of Jesus as a troublemaker before the Romans came and violently destroyed the entire nation. John saw the phrase "die for the people" as a prophecy regarding the atoning nature of Jesus' death. His death for the people signified the fact that he died for their sins so that they would not perish eternally. John added the comment, "Now this he did not say on his own initiative; but being high priest that year, he prophesied that Jesus was going to die for the nation; and not for the nation only, but that He might also gather together into one the children of God who are scattered abroad" (11:51-52). This quotation by the high priest is an example of irony, which occurs several times in John. Irony is a way of speaking in which something opposite to the literal meaning of the words is implied. Here the high priest spoke words with deeper meaning than he himself knew.

The Anointing at Bethany (12:1-8)

Jesus sat at table in Bethany, and Mary anointed the feet of Jesus and wiped his feet with her hair. The key to the incident is Jesus' defense of what Mary did in spending precious ointment in this way. He said, "Let her alone, in order that she may keep it for the day of My burial" (12:7). Jesus, foreseeing his death, interpreted the anointing as a kind of last rite in preparation for his burial. Mary would keep her act of devotion in her memory, remembering that she had in this way expressed her love for Jesus while he was still with them. By this act, then, the death of Jesus is foreshadowed.

The Triumphal Entry into Jerusalem (12:12-19)

The so-called "triumph" of Jesus' entry is short-lived in the Gospels. Jesus was indeed king, and he deserved a royal entrance. That honor would not be his, however, until after the resurrection. He would then have conquered death, sin, and Satan. He would then be the Lord of life. Someone has suggested that the triumphal entry, too, has a prophetic meaning. It foreshadowed the triumph which rightfully belonged to Jesus and which was ultimately to be his. Even now, in our day and age, his reign is a hidden one, recognized only by believers. The day will come when every knee will bow and every tongue confess that Jesus Christ is Lord (Philippians 2:9-11).

Jesus' Public Ministry Comes to a Close (12:20-50)

This section begins with the appearance of "the Greeks" at the Feast of the Passover. The expression "the Greeks" seems to refer to Gentiles, that is, non-Jews. Their coming marked the arrival of Jesus' "hour." His hour was the time God had determined when Jesus should give his life on the cross so that salvation might be possible for all people. Jesus' death on the cross was not for John a moment of defeat but, rather, the hour of "glory." It was the hour of glory because it fulfilled the plan of God. It manifested the love of God for the world, and it marked the culmination of a life of total obedience to the Father which Jesus lived while on earth. In the rest of the New Testament glory is associated with the resurrection of Jesus (compare Philippians 2:9-11). John moved from the obvious to the not so obvious. He thought in terms of the eternal plan of God for humankind's redemption. Jesus interpreted his death side by side with the thought of glorification. He said, "The hour has come for the Son of Man to be glorified. Truly, truly, I say to you, unless a grain of wheat falls into the earth and dies, it remains by itself alone; but if it dies, it bears much fruit" (John 12:23-24).

The coming of the Greeks marked this transition. Until then, Jesus' ministry had been directed almost exclusively toward the Jews. It was after his death that the church embraced the Gentile mission. Then the gospel was preached freely to Jews and Gentiles alike. The time had come for Jesus to consummate the work for which he had come to earth. This included "the gather[ing] together into one" of "the children of God," both Jew and Gentile (11:52). This included "the other sheep" (10:16). Paul was later to write, "There is neither Jew nor Greek . . . for you are all one in Christ Jesus" (Galatians 3:28).

When Jesus says in John 12:32, "And I, if I be lifted up from the earth, will draw all men to Myself," he is referring not to the ascension, but to the crucifixion. John makes this clear by his added comment, "But He was saying this to indicate the kind of death by which He was to die" (12:33). John uses similar terminology in 3:14.

Conclusion to the Book of Signs

There are two parts to this section: (1) the writer's summary (12:37-43) and (2) a final invitation and warning by Jesus (12:44-50). In John's summary he reports that despite the many signs performed by Jesus, many did not believe on him. This, he says, had been predicted by the prophet Isaiah. John criticizes those who refuse to confess Jesus for fear of possible persecution. He voices the following sharp criticism: "They loved the approval of men rather than the approval of God" (12:43). These words may well have a double thrust in the intention of John. They speak, on the one hand, of what some people have already done. On the other hand, John may intend them to be words of admonition addressed to the readers of his Gospel. There are some of them who may be in similar situations. He is therefore indirectly saying to them, "Do not be like these persons, who put self-concern ahead of devotion to God. Step out, whatever the cost, and let your belief in Jesus as the Christ be known. In that way you will have God's approval." It is a kind of final appeal on the part of John to his readers.

The final paragraph (12:44-50) is not in John's words but is given over to a statement made by Jesus. The occasion or location of this saying in the ministry of Jesus is not identified. It is almost as if John wishes Jesus to have "the last word" before the Book of Signs comes to a close. Jesus' words include an invitation, a promise, and a warning. If we examine the contents of this short paragraph, we find a concise summary of the teachings of Jesus and of the whole Book of Signs. It gives in a nutshell what has been proclaimed in the entire first part of John. The main statements may be summarized as follows:

1. To believe in Jesus is to believe in God the Father who sent him. Jesus comes with God's authority behind him.
2. Jesus' purpose in coming into the world was redemptive. He came to bring people out of darkness into light.
3. Those who reject Jesus will be judged on the last day. They will not be judged by Jesus, but by the very words of truth and life which God the Father gave Jesus to give to them.
4. Finally, the readers are reminded that it is a life-and-death issue. Those who believe in Jesus Christ find eternal life. It was for this reason that Jesus came into the world. John's emphasis on this fact makes it very appropriate to call this Gospel "The Gospel of Life."

Life Transformed

At the Last Supper the disciples were not seated on chairs, as shown in Leonardo da Vinci's famous painting. They reclined, instead, on low couches around a table, as was the custom of the times. The word which our Bibles translate as "seated" is actually in the Greek "reclined." The location of the upper room where Jesus met for the last time with his disciples is on what is now called Mount Zion. According to a fourth-century writer named Epiphanius, the emperor Hadrian, when he visited Jerusalem in A.D. 135, found the building of which the upper room was a part still standing and venerated by Christians. Through the centuries various pilgrims to Jerusalem continued to refer to visits to the upper room. The upper room is often called the Cenacle, which comes from the Latin and means "dining room."

The original building has now disappeared, but there stands on the traditional site a building remodeled from a fourteenth-century church. This structure has two floors, In the sixteenth century the lower floor was turned into a Moslem mosque. Today this area has been turned into a Jewish memorial to King David. The upper room is now reached by means of an outside staircase which has deep grooves worn into it by the countless thousands who have come here to remember the place where Jesus ate his last meal with his disciples before his death. While the present building is not the original one, it is built on the traditional site of the one in which Jesus met with his disciples. Deep emotions are often stirred in the hearts of modern visitors to places, such as this one, which are full of memories about the life, teachings, and ministry of Jesus. In many ways the Bible takes on new meaning, vitality, and interest through experiences like this. It is like going back in time to walk in the places where so many of the events described in our Bible took place. We must remember, of course, that Jesus is not now in any way tied to geography. Through the resurrection and the gift of the Holy Spirit to the church, Jesus can be present with us in our own country just as much as he can be in some distant land like Israel. He promised his disciples that where two or three gather in his name, there he would meet with them through his Spirit (Matthew 18:20). Nevertheless, a visit to some of these places where Jesus once walked and taught can have a most moving and enriching impact upon our understanding of and appreciation for the biblical narratives.

The upper room discourse in John includes chapters 13–17. This discourse begins what has been called the Book of Glory (John 13:1–20:31). This entire section focuses on the suffering of Jesus and on his instructions to his disciples given in the light of his coming death and departure from them.

The Last Supper (13:1-38)

Just before his betrayal and trial Jesus met with his disciples for a final meal. Chapter 13 opens with the words, "Now before the Feast of the Passover, Jesus knowing that His hour had come that He should depart out of this world to the Father . . . ." "His hour" refers to his crucifixion and resurrection. The shadow of the cross is therefore present at the very outset of the discourse. What is subsequently said by Jesus is said in the light of that coming event. This part of the Gospel of John is, therefore, to be regarded as Jesus' farewell discourse and may be compared to the farewell discourse of Jacob to his sons (Genesis 49). The words are addressed specifically to Jesus' "own" (John 13:1), that is, his disciples. The expression "his own" has two meanings in John. In John 1:11b it refers to fellow members of the Jewish people. There we read, "He came to His own, and those who were His own did not receive Him." The first phrase can be rendered, "His own things, possessions, domain," as indicated in the marginal note of the *New American Standard Bible.* The second phrase, however, refers to the Jewish people. In John 13:1 the use of the words "His own" refers not to the Jews in general but to those persons who believed in Jesus and had become his followers. We should, therefore, regard the upper room discourse as addressed to believers and not to the world. Whereas in the Book of Signs (1:19-12:50) Jesus revealed his glory to the world, in this section he reveals his glory to the church. For John, what Jesus says to the disciples, he also says through them to the readers of the Gospel and to the church at large. *We,* the members of the church today, are now his people and it is to *us,* therefore, as twentieth-century disciples that these words are appropriately applied.

When it says that Jesus loved them "to the end" (13:1), this can mean "utterly, completely," or it can mean "to the point of death." The first possibility, which stresses the quality of Jesus' love, is most appropriate. This is well expressed in the translation given for this phrase by *The New English Bible.* It reads, "He had always loved his own who were in the world, and now he was to show the full extent of his love."

The Foot Washing

Many of the actions of Jesus surprised people. He ate with tax collectors and with the common people of the land. He healed on the sabbath day. He ate food without first ceremonially washing his hands, as the Pharisees did. He defended his disciples when they ate some grain they had taken from a field while walking through it on the sabbath day. He dared to reinterpret the Law and to call into question traditions which were long established in Judaism. One of the things which surprised the disciples the most, however, was his decision to wash their feet at the supper. This was normally a servant's task. That Jesus performed it symbolized his whole life-style. By this act Jesus demonstrated what he had earlier taught, namely, "For even the Son of Man did not come to be served, but to serve, and to give His life a ransom for many" (Mark 10:45). The other Gospels do not mention this action of foot washing by Jesus. Luke, however, has Jesus at the Last Supper speak words which would have been appropriate for such an act. A dispute had arisen among the disciples as to who should be regarded as the leader of them. Jesus rebuked them for their egoism and said, ". . . let him who is the greatest among you become as the youngest, and the leader as the servant. For who is greater, the one who reclines at table, or the one who serves? Is it not the one who reclines at table? But I am among you as the one who serves" (Luke 22:26-27).

What did Jesus really seek to teach by his self-denying act of washing the feet of the disciples? What lessons does it carry for us in the twentieth century? This incident has probably greater meaning than many of us have recognized. Let us think of its significance.

1. *By his act of washing their feet, Jesus predicted and symbolized the fact that through his coming death on the cross they would be cleansed from their sins.*

This lesson has often not been recognized by Christian interpreters. That it is a valid interpretation, however, is supported by what Jesus said to Peter when the disciple protested against Jesus' actions. Jesus said, "If I do not wash you, you have no part with Me" (John 13:8*b*). How does Jesus wash us? True spiritual washing has nothing to do with water and feet. It involves a cleansing of the soul. This was accomplished through the fact that Jesus bore our sins on the tree for us, as we read in First Peter, "He Himself bore our sins in His body on the cross, that we might die to sin and live to righteousness; for by His wounds you were healed" (1 Peter 2:24). Jesus recognized that at that moment in the upper room the meaning of what he was doing would not be clear to Peter. It would become obvious to Peter only after the cross, when Jesus would have accomplished the task for which he came. For this reason Jesus said to Peter, "What I do you do not realize now; but you shall understand hereafter" (John 13:7). Merrill C. Tenney adds the appropriate comment, "Later the meaning would be intelligible in the light of the cross which provided a cleansing for all men, without which no one could have a part in the heritage of the saints."[1]

Leon Morris has also remarked that Jesus meant more than foot washing when he said that Peter needed to be washed if he were to "have a part," that is, find acceptance and fellowship, with Jesus. Morris writes: "But Jesus means more. A literal washing of the feet is not necessary before a man can be a Christian. The words point us to a washing free from sin which only Christ can give. Apart from this a man will have no part in Christ."[2]

2. *By washing his disciples' feet, Jesus gave them an example and an exhortation to adopt a life-style of service to others.*

That the incident carries this meaning is clear from Jesus' statement, "If I then, the Lord and the Teacher, washed your feet, you also ought to wash one another's feet. For I gave you an example that you also should do as I did to you. Truly, truly, I say to you, a slave is not greater than his master; neither one who is sent greater than the one who sent him" (13:14-16).

There are those who practice foot washing today. The pope washes the feet of selected poor persons on Maundy Thursday as a symbolic act of humility. Some Protestant denominations, such as the Church of the Brethren, make it a part of their Communion service. Perhaps more important than the actual practice of foot washing is the life-style to which it points. The apostle Paul reminded his readers that they should be willing to serve others, even as Jesus did in his earthly ministry (Philippians 2:5-8).

Dietrich Bonhoeffer put it well when he said, "The cross is laid on every Christian. The first Christ-suffering which every man must experience is the call to abandon the attachments of this world. It is that dying of the old man which is the result of his encounter with Christ. . . . When Christ calls a man, he bids him come and die."[3]

We might well ask what it means to "wash a brother's feet" in our day and age. To such a question Bonhoeffer gave the answer: "As Christ bears our burdens, so ought we to bear the burdens of our fellow-men. . . . But how is the disciple to know what kind of cross is meant for him? He will find out as soon as he begins to follow his Lord and to share his life."[4]

3. *By washing the disciples' feet, Jesus indicated that even disciples need cleansing from defilement which results from their daily walk in the world.*

This interpretation emerges from the little phrase "needs only to wash his feet" (13:10). A Swiss pastor applied these words in this way: "We may have received forgiveness for our sins once and for all, nevertheless we frequently need to be forgiven anew because we go on sinning day after day. We may have entered irrevocably into the love of Jesus Christ. Nevertheless we need His love for us to be renewed again and again."[5]

This comment is certainly in keeping with what the New Testament teaches about the need for Christians to confess their sins to God and to have them forgiven. It was to Christians that the following statement was written: "If we say that we have no sin, we are deceiving ourselves, and the truth is not in us. If we confess our sins, He is faithful and righteous to forgive us our sins and to cleanse us from all unrighteousness" (1 John 1:8-9).

Some early Greek manuscripts omit the phrase "except for his feet," and on this basis these words are not included in *The New English Bible* which renders this verse in the following way: "Jesus said, 'A man who has bathed needs no further washing; he is altogether clean; and you are clean, though not every one of you'" (John 13:10).

Before we leave the foot-washing scene, it is of interest to note that Raymond E. Brown translates the word "basin" as "pitcher." His translation of John 13:5 reads, "Then he poured water into a pitcher and began to wash his disciples' feet and to dry them with the towel he had around him."[6] The Greek word is *nipter*. This word comes from *nipto,* meaning "to wash" and therefore means "a vessel used for washing." The context has to determine how we should translate it. In the Near East washing was consistently done by pouring water over parts of the body, not by washing in a basin of standing water. An example would be the account of Elisha's service to Elijah. Concerning this we read, "Elisha the son of Shaphat is here, who used to pour water on the hands of Elijah" (2 Kings 3:11). Jesus did not wash the disciples' feet in a basin. The disciples were reclining on couches, and their feet were therefore away from the table at the outer edge of the circle. Jesus went around the circle and poured water over their feet. The water was collected in a bowl which may have had a cover pierced with holes. In this way the soiled water disappeared from view through the strainer into the bottom of the basin. We should think of the *nipter* then as a jug, with a basin held under it to catch the water as it was poured out over the feet.[7]

"Love one another" (13:34)

Jesus repeats this commandment in 15:12. Note the stress on a "new" commandment. This reminds us of the wording which Jesus used when he instituted the Lord's Supper. He said, "This cup is the new covenant in My blood . . ." (1 Corinthians 11:25). Only to those who have come to share in the new covenant has this new commandment been given.

Love plays such an important part in the Gospel According to John that the apostle John is often called "the apostle of love." This emphasis appears to be the foundation of everything else in terms of Christian ethics. It is more than an emotional feeling toward others. Genuine love results in positive actions on behalf of our brothers and sisters in need. We find this stressed in First John, where we read,

"But whoever has the world's goods, and beholds his brother in need and closes his heart against him, how does the love of God abide in him? Little children, let us not love with word or with tongue, but in deed and truth" (1 John 3:17-18). By demonstrating love to one another, the believers will show to the world around them that they are participants in a *new* community which has been founded through the *new* covenant established by Jesus Christ (see John 13:35).

Regarding the deep need for Christians to love, Walter Lüthi in his book entitled *St. John's Gospel* makes the following moving comment:

> There are so many gardens of life in which no flower blooms any more, and no bird sings, and in which the fruit of charity will never ripen again. Come and let these barren gardens be replanted, for Christ wants flowers to bloom and birds to sing in them again and the fruits of brotherly love to thrive. For "By this shall all men know that ye are my disciples, if ye have love one to another."[8]

Why does the Gospel According to John talk about loving the brethren but not about loving the neighbor, as in Luke 10:27, which echoes Leviticus 19:18? The reason for this is that in the upper room discourse Jesus gave instructions regarding the proper relationship which needs to exist between believers. At this point Jesus was not talking about the world. That the Gospel According to John also has this wider concern in mind is clear from the love of God for the world (John 3:16); from the recognition that Jesus is the Savior of the world (4:42); from the command to be witnesses to the world (15:27); and from Jesus' commission of the disciples, as he sent them forth to minister in his name (20:21). John's concern is as broad as that of the other Gospel writers. It is just that these particular words are addressed to believers, and their primary theme focuses on the proper relationship which should exist between disciples within the fellowship of the church.

Selfishness and self-centeredness can spoil our lives, too. These words of Jesus in John 13:34 can serve like a lighthouse on a rocky coast. Its beacon reaches out into the darkness to warn us that a self-centered life can shipwreck God's plans for our lives. By letting love rule within us, we can find our way through life's treacherous waters. As God's love directs our lives, we will by his grace radiate that love both to our brother within the fellowship and to our neighbor outside of it.

"I will come again" (14:1-31)

In this chapter Jesus promises his disciples that he will do two things for them, namely,

1. Jesus will prepare a place for them in the Father's house to which he will take them (14:1-3), and
2. Jesus will come with the Father to the believers through the Holy Spirit in order to make their home or dwelling with them (14:23).

There is, therefore, a two-fold promise. The first promise looks ahead into eternity; the other gives reassurance to believers who are concerned that they will be left as orphans in the world after Jesus' departure.

The opening verse of the chapter can be translated either "Let not your heart be troubled; ye believe in God, believe also in me," or as "Let not your heart be troubled; believe in God, believe also in Me." The Greek would be the same in either case. The King James Version has the first interpretation; the New American Standard Version has the second. The phrase in question could even be rendered as a question. It would then read, "Do you believe in God? Then believe also in me."

Charles B. Williams, who seeks to stay close to the original in his translation, has this helpful rendering: "Stop letting your hearts be troubled; keep on believing in God, and also in me."

The Father's House (14:2)

In this verse the King James Version has the following phrase, "In my Father's house are many mansions." The word translated "mansions" is the Greek word *mone,* and it means literally "abiding places" or "dwelling places." The only other verse where this word occurs in the New Testament is in this same chapter in verse 23 where we are told that Jesus and the Father will come to the believer and make their "abode ["dwelling," NEB] with him." The noun *mone* is related to the Greek verb *menein,* which means to "remain" or "abide." This is the verb that is used in John's next chapter when he quotes the words of Jesus, "Abide in Me, and I in you . . ." (15:4). The word *mone* does not describe the nature of the place which has been prepared for us. Instead it describes its function, namely, it tells us that God has provided for us a home, residence, or dwelling place for eternity; and that place, we are told, is in the presence of God.

Communion, fellowship, joy—these are the implications of these words. The main thought here is that in the age to come we shall be in the presence of our heavenly Father. We can leave the details up to God, the Creator of the universe. The words of Paul are helpful at this point. He wrote, "But, in the words of Scripture, 'Things beyond our seeing, things beyond our hearing, things beyond our imagining, all prepared by God for those who love him,' these it is that God has revealed to us through the Spirit" (1 Corinthians 2:9-10, NEB).

"I am the way, and the truth, and the life" (14:6)

The words "true" and "truth" are favorite words in the Gospel According to John. He uses them forty-eight times, while Matthew, Mark, and Luke use them only ten times, in total. For John, Jesus is the giver, source, and very being of truth (1:14, 17; 14:6). Jesus bears witness to the truth (18:37) and speaks the truth (8:40, 45-46; 16:7). The truth sets the disciples free (8:32). The Holy Spirit is given the unique name "the Spirit of truth" (14:17; 15:26; 16:13).

To worship "in spirit and truth" (4:24) means to worship God through the One who is the truth, namely Jesus Christ. John has a gift for dramatic situations. We see this once more as Jesus stands before Pilate and Pilate says to him, "What is truth?" (18:38). Pilate breaks off the conversation at this point. He asks what truth is, and Truth stands before him!

"He who has seen Me has seen the Father" (14:9)

Jesus does not here say that he is the Father. The statement means that in the person and life of Jesus, God the Father has been most perfectly revealed. If we want to know what God is like, we are invited to look with care at Jesus his Son, whom God sent into the world in order to manifest the Father among humankind (1:14).

"Greater works than these shall he do" (14:12)

Since Jesus raised the dead, among other miracles, how can we understand a verse like this which was addressed to all the disciples? The emphasis is on the fact that they will become effective witnesses through the gift of the Holy Spirit. As Leon Morris writes, "The emphasis is on the mighty works of conversion. On the day of Pentecost alone more believers were added to the little band of believers than throughout Christ's entire earthly life."[9]

"Whatever you ask in My name, that will I do" (14:13)

Jesus was not giving the disciples a blank check which they could fill out any way their whims might dictate. We must first be in the Lord's will; then our requests will be in harmony with God's will. Regarding the nature of the requests to which Jesus had referred, Raymond E. Brown has this helpful observation: "They are requests of such a nature that when they are granted the Father is glorified in the Son. . . . They are requests pertinent to the Christian life and to the continuation of the work by which Jesus glorified the Father during his ministry (17:4)." [10] Our prayers need to be like those of Jesus who prayed, "Not My will, but thine be done" (Luke 22:42).

Life in Christ

In British Columbia, Canada, the Frazer River is famous because of the sockeye salmon which come there every year and fight their way upstream more than seven hundred miles to spawn in the shallower and quieter waters east of the Alaska panhandle. They fight rapids, leap high waterfalls, and face preying bears, as by instinct they return to the stream where they themselves were born. Enough of them make the trip successfully to guarantee the supply of new salmon for the following year. The struggle of the salmon to reach their destination is not unlike our endeavor as Christians to persevere in discipleship. Fortunately we are not alone in our efforts. In the chapter which we are now going to study, we are told that we are part of "the vine," that is, Jesus Christ. As we "abide" in him, we find the strength to meet successfully the challenges of daily living (John 15:4).

The Pattern for Christian Living (15:1-27)

In this chapter three dimensions of the believer's life are described in turn. They are:

1. the believer's relationship to Jesus (15:1-11),
2. the believer's relationship to other believers (15:12-17),

3. the believer's relationship to the world (15:18-27).

In a nutshell we can summarize these relationships as follows:

1. The believer is to *abide* in Christ (15:4).
2. The believer is to *love* the brethren (15:12).
3. The believer is to *keep separate* from the values of the world which are alien to God, but is at the same time to *bear witness* to the world concerning Jesus who represents an alternate value system and life-style (15:18, 27).

The Image of the Vine

In the Old Testament the imagery of the vine is often used for Israel. Israel is called a vine which God took from Egypt and planted on the fertile soil of the Promised Land. The psalmist writes:

> Thou didst remove a vine from Egypt;
> Thou didst drive out the nations, and didst plant it.
> Thou didst clear the ground before it,
> And it took deep root and filled the land.
> The mountains were covered with its shadow;
> And the cedars of God with its boughs.
> It was sending out its branches to the sea,
> And its shoots to the River.
>
> Psalm 80:8-11

Similar passages are Isaiah 5:1-2, 7; 27:2-6; Jeremiah 2:21; 12:10; Ezekiel 15:2-8; 19:10-14. The vine has become a symbol for Israel as a nation. In the time of the Maccabees, who in the second century B.C. obtained political freedom for the Jews, coins were minted that had the impression of a vine stamped on them. In Jesus' day a great golden vine had been fashioned by skilled workmen as a decoration for the entrance to the Holy Place of the temple. In Israel today the Israeli tourist service has as its emblem a very large cluster of grapes carried on a pole between two men, reminiscent of the grapes of Eshcol which the spies brought back from their trip into Canaan (Numbers 13:23).

When Jesus adopted this ancient imagery for his own followers, he explained through a parable how this could be (Mark 12:1-9). It is the parable of the owner of a vineyard who was so disappointed by the unfaithful behavior of his tenants that he decided to get new tenants. He himself, according to the parable, had to go away on a journey. He periodically sent servants back in order to receive his proper share of the profits. All of the servants were mistreated and sent away empty-handed. Some of them were killed. Finally, the rich man sent his son. He, too, was killed. This parable Jesus told against the religious leaders in Israel, and he viewed his own rejection by these leaders as the rejection of the son who had come to represent his father. Jesus concluded his parable with the words: "What will the owner of the vineyard do? He will come and destroy the vine-growers, and will give the vineyard to others" (Mark 12:9). In keeping with this theme of poor and good tenants of the vineyard, Jesus began his present parable of the vine with the words, "I am the *true* vine . . . " (John 15:1, italics added). Israel, as a vine, had not brought forth good fruit but had become "a foreign vine" (Jeremiah 2:21) and had produced worthless grapes (see Isaiah 5:2). What Jesus was doing was not very different from what the Old Testament prophets had done in their criticism of Israel. The unique factor is that Jesus added the statement that now, at that time, God was acting dramatically through him to establish a whole new order of things. The new age had dawned, and with it the offer of the kingdom was being made to the poor, the blind, the lame, the harlot, and the publican, not just to the righteous and respected members of society. With the coming of Jesus the new age had come. The adjective "true" was deliberately chosen in order to contrast Jesus with the fruitless vine of Israel. God had created a new thing, namely, the church.

The symbol of the vine stresses the organic unity of the church. All of the life, vitality, and fruitfulness of the branches come through the vine. We are to abide in Christ, and his words are to abide in us (John 15:7). In this way we shall bear much fruit.

In transferring the image of the vine from Israel to Christ and the church, we see the New Testament development of the idea of the church as the new Israel. Similarly in 1 Peter 2:9, terms which in the Old Testament were consistently applied to Israel were taken over and applied to the church. There we read: "But you are A CHOSEN RACE, A ROYAL PRIESTHOOD, A HOLY NATION, . . . GOD'S OWN POSSESSION. . . ." All of these terms are terms for Israel in the Old Testament. Since Jesus is the vine and we are the branches, we need to realize that we, too, are a part of the vine. After all, a vine consists not only in the stalk, but in the branches as well. Just as the image of the vine is used of Israel collectively in the Old Testament, so this image is used in this passage of the church collectively.

"Abide in Me" (15:4)

This command can also be translated "dwell in me" or "remain in me." John tells us that we abide in Jesus as we keep Jesus' commandments. It is then that we will bear fruit. John does not define the nature of this fruit bearing. Presumably, fruit bearing is every demonstration of vitality of faith and of Christian service. Sometimes fruit in the New Testament is maturity of Christian character (Matthew 3:8; 7:20; Galatians 5:22-23; Ephesians 5:9; Philippians 1:11). Love of the brethren would certainly for John be at the heart of fruitfulness. From and through the vine must flow that life-giving quality which is necessary for our spiritual health and productivity. For apart from Jesus, we are told, we can do nothing (John 15:5). By bearing "much fruit," we prove that we truly are disciples of Jesus. Leon Morris comments, "That discipleship is not static, but a growing and developing way of life. Always the true disciple is becoming more fully a disciple." [1] He adds that abiding in Christ's love does not involve some mystical experience. It is simple obedience that is called for. Jesus makes this clear by his statement in chapter 15 verse 10, "If you keep My commandments, you will abide in My love" (15:10).

Some Branches Are Taken Away and Some Are Pruned

This is the observation made in 15:2. The Father clears away the unprofitable branches, and he prunes those that bear fruit. Two separate actions by the gardener are here described. Branches that cannot bear fruit are cut off in Israel in the months of February and March. Later in August, when there has been considerable growth, there is a second pruning. This time the little shoots are pinched off so that the main fruit-bearing branches get the important nourishment they need to bear well. In the lives of believers there remain areas that are not under the Lord's control, and these need to be trimmed by the Lord.

There is a play on words in the Greek between the words "take away" and "prune." The word for "take away" is *airei;* the word for "prune" is *kathairei.* When the two words are spoken, they have a similar sound to the ear.

Calvin makes this observation about the meaning of the verse: "... believers need incessant culture, that they may be prevented from degenerating ... for it will not be enough to have been once made partakers of adoption, if God does not continue the work of his grace in us."[2] The price of spiritual victory and fruitfulness in our lives is nothing less than constant abiding.

Chosen for Fruit Bearing (15:16)

God has chosen his disciples through Jesus, not for privilege and honor, but for fruit bearing. When the fruit is not present, we are not fulfilling the purpose for which we have been called. In what ways can we bear fruit? Some monks withdraw to distant monasteries and there give themselves to prayer, study, and meditation. While this may be God's calling for a few, it certainly is not his calling to most of us. Jesus did not withdraw from society, except for brief periods of time to rest and pray. Then he would return in order to minister to his generation. Each one of us needs to seek God's specific call to his or her life. We should by prayer, the Scriptures, and the guidance of the Holy Spirit in our own lives and in the lives of the community of faith seek to know the Lord's will.

At times the Christian battle is a battle against the stream. It calls for perseverance, determination, and effort. Christians are not alone. We are united with the vine. We are united with Christ, and in our battle we have his strength and presence to encourage and sustain us. Abide in him, and he will abide in you. We abide in him when we keep his commandments. When this happens, we will bear fruit, and this will demonstrate to the world that we are indeed his disciples.

When the Counselor Comes (15:26)

The Gospel of John places much more stress on the Holy Spirit than do the other three Gospels. It has even been given the title "The Gospel of the Spirit." Key passages are the following: 1:33; 7:39; 14:15-26; 15:26; 16:7-15; 20:22. Jesus is anointed by the Spirit for his ministry (1:33). He is the one who gives the Spirit to the believer (7:39; 20:22). When the Spirit comes, both the Father and the Son come to dwell with the believer (14:18-23). The birth from above is through the Spirit (3:5-6). The birth thus begun needs the continuing presence of the Spirit to bring it to maturity. When the Spirit comes, he will be five things:

1. Helper (14:15-17),
2. Teacher (14:25-26),
3. Witness (15:26),
4. Judge (16:4-11),
5. Guide (16:12-15).

The Holy Spirit as the Paraclete

The word translated "Comforter" in the King James Version is *parakletos.* This is sometimes rendered in English (without seeking to translate it) as "Paraclete." It is found in John 14:16, 26; 15:26; and 16:7. The only other place where it is found in the Bible is in 1 John 2:1, where it refers not to the Holy Spirit but to Christ. The translation "Comforter" goes back to the translation made in the fourteenth century by John Wycliffe. The word then had a meaning which was closely connected with its Latin root *fortis,* meaning "brave, strong, courageous." To see in this name for the Paraclete only the ideas of comfort, consolation, and sympathy is to miss the Spirit's role as strengthener, enabler, helper. It was the Spirit who gave to the disheartened apostles the courage and strength to speak boldly for Christ and to triumph over the dangers and opposition, both physical and spiritual, which confronted them. The translation "Helper" in the New American Standard Version captures the central thought very well. Weymouth and *The New English Bible* use the translation "Advocate." This literally renders the meaning of the Greek, which actually is "someone called alongside to help." This is what the Latin *advocatus* also suggests ("ad" plus "vocare"—literally, "to call to"). The advocate is one who pleads the cause of another. He also is an intercessor. Compare here 1 John 2:1. The nature of the Spirit's help is wider than the image which the law court might suggest. Just what that help is can best be determined by examining the passages which tell of his coming.

Old Testament Background

In the Old Testament no distinction was drawn between God and the Spirit. The Holy Spirit was God as he was active in his world. We see the Spirit active, for example, in creation (Genesis 1:2). The Spirit anointed men for special ministry (Genesis 41:38; Judges 6:34). Through the Spirit men spoke for God (2 Samuel 23:2; compare 2 Peter 1:21). The Holy Spirit was not so much a daily power and presence as he was an unusual endowment for a specific duty or responsibility.

There are two important passages which clearly identify the Spirit with the Presence of God. These passages are written in the form of Hebrew parallelism, which was the way in which Hebrew poetry was structured. In these examples the two lines of poetry in each case are but two ways of saying the same thing. This means that each line has the same meaning and that they can be more or less equated—one helps to explain or clarify the other. The verses read:

> Do not cast me away from *Thy presence,*
> And do not take *Thy Holy Spirit* from me.
> Psalm 51:11

> Where can I go from *Thy Spirit?*
> Or where can I flee from *Thy presence?*
> Psalm 139:7

The italics in each case are mine. They serve to show the correspondence between the lines. In the above verses the Spirit of God is clearly equated with God's Presence.

Matthew, Mark, and Luke

References to the Spirit in the Synoptic Gospels (Matthew, Mark, and Luke) are not nearly as frequent as they are in John and in the writings of Paul, where the doctrine and teaching of the Spirit are more fully developed. Many of the references in the Synoptics are directly connected with the life of Jesus himself: he was conceived by the Holy Spirit (Luke 1:35); the Spirit came on him at his baptism (Matthew 3:16); he was led by the Spirit into the wilderness (Matthew 4:1); he returned from the Jordan to begin his ministry "full of the Holy Spirit" (Luke 4:1); by the Spirit he cast out demons (Matthew 12:28); and it was by the Spirit that he was anointed to preach the gospel to the poor (Luke 4:18; Isaiah 61:1-2). Finally, we have the promise expressed by Luke, "And behold, I am sending forth the promise of My Father upon you; but you are to stay in the city until you are clothed with power from on high" (Luke 24:49). This promise is repeated in Luke's second volume, the book of Acts, where we read, "But you shall receive power when the Holy Spirit has come upon you; and you shall be My witnesses both in Jerusalem, and in all Judea and Samaria and even to the remotest part of the earth" (Acts 1:8).

The Synoptic Gospels were written from the perspective of anticipation of the Spirit. The Gospel of John consciously reflects an awareness that now the Spirit *has been given* to the church, and the author seeks to instruct the believers more fully regarding the importance, nature, and work of the Holy Spirit who has been given to them.

The Importance of the Spirit

All Christian experience is based both on Christ and upon the Spirit of God. It is only through the Spirit that we can live the Christian life successfully. In the early church the Spirit was a central reality. Long before he became an article of faith or doctrine, he was a dynamic and vital reality in the life and experience of the early church. We are living in a time when there is renewed interest in the Spirit and in his work. Through the Spirit a new vitality can come to the twentieth-century church.

"And He, when He comes, will convict the world concerning sin, and righteousness, and judgment" (16:8)

The word rendered "convict" carries the connotation of "to prove guilty." In this verse we are told that the Spirit will do three things:

1. He will prove to the disciples that the world is guilty of sin, basically of the sin of refusing to believe in Jesus.
2. He will prove that the world was wrong about justice, for he will show that Jesus, whom the world declared to be guilty, was actually innocent and just.
3. He will demonstrate that in the very act of condemning Jesus, the world itself was judged. In rejecting the Light, the true darkness in which the world existed was thereby made manifest.

Through this ministry of the Spirit, there is a clear disclosure of who is the sinner, who is the victor, and who it is that is judged. What a reversal of the standards and values of the world is here revealed!

"But when He, the Spirit of truth, comes . . ." (16:13)

The expression "Spirit of truth," while used only in the Gospel of John and First John in the Bible, is one which was also current among the Essenes who produced the Dead Sea Scrolls. John uses this expression in 14:17; 15:26; 16:13; and 1 John 4:6. In the last reference we have the spirit of truth contrasted to the spirit of error. Similarly, in the Scrolls we have the contrast between the spirit of truth and the spirit of deceit. The similarity is probably not the result of direct influence in either direction. Both reflect a common Hebraic heritage.

"He will guide you into all the truth . . ." (16:13)

Jesus promised that the Spirit would guide the disciples. It is the same for us as it was for the early disciples. What the Spirit shares with the disciples is not primarily new content but a new understanding of what Christ has already done and said. In Jesus there is embodied the full revelation of God, and the Spirit continually leads us into new and fresh understandings of the implications of that truth. Frequently in John we are told that some event in the life of Christ was not fully understood until after Jesus' resurrection. These would be examples of the "truth" into which the Spirit guides the disciples. See John 2:22; 12:16; 13:7. Since Jesus is the revelation of the Father, any further light will be in keeping with this foundational truth.

At the same time we may see in this verse an important explanation by the writer himself of why the Gospel of John differs in so many remarkable ways from the Synoptics. Here we have not only what Jesus said but also the meaning of his life and work. In John's Gospel at least three elements appear to have been closely interwoven. First of all, there are the events of Jesus' life as they have been recalled and retold through the intervening decades. Secondly, for several decades there has been reflection by the church upon the meaning of Jesus Christ and of his gospel as it has been shared and studied, first in Palestine and then in the cities of Asia Minor. Finally, there has been the guidance of the Holy Spirit. The Spirit has led Christ's followers into all the truth. John is convinced of this, and for this reason he can write with such authority and persuasiveness.

We have a picture which is more than just a recounting of events. It has been molded and shaped by the work of the Spirit on the lives of the author and his fellow believers. The author is a portrait painter. He is concerned to interpret, to give meaning, to set into perspective these great events which had lately taken place and which thereafter changed the course of history for all time.

"He shall glorify me . . ." (16:14)

The Spirit will always point to Christ and reveal the essential nature and person of Christ. He will help believers to understand these truths which to the natural mind so often seem to be mere foolishness (1 Corinthians 1:18-25). It is only through the departure of Christ that the Spirit can come. When the Spirit comes, Christ also comes and takes up his residence with us. Christ has not forgotten his church. He who said, "I will not leave you as orphans; I will come to you" (John 14:18) remains through his Spirit with his church. It was the Spirit of *Jesus* (this is the reading in the *New American Standard*

Bible, The New English Bible, and the Revised Standard Version for Acts 16:7) that led the apostles in the task of carrying out the mission of the church. We do not need to seek Christ amid the olive trees in the garden of Gethsemane or at any of the countless shrines that dot the Holy Land. Wherever the true church is, there is the risen Christ in its midst. We have the further promise that the Spirit of Jesus will be the companion and guide of each believer.

In stressing that the Father and the Son come to dwell with the believer through the Spirit (John 14:18-23), John does not lose sight of the Second Coming of Christ. He speaks of this in 14:3. This ultimate coming, however, does not take away from John's stress on the fact that in one sense Jesus has returned already and is now present with his church in the person of the Spirit. Perhaps this teaching was a needed corrective in John's day. It may be that too many were looking to the day of Christ's Second Coming and were putting such stress on it that they had a sense of being orphans and left alone. Not so, says John; Christ is with us here and now, and we must be responsive to his continued leading day by day.

The Holy Spirit Today

In a dramatic way there has developed a new interest in the Spirit in our generation. The Spirit is important because it is through him that we are born from above. This is where our spiritual life begins. As the apostle Paul once wrote, "But if anyone does not have the Spirit of Christ, he does not belong to Him" (Romans 8:9b). As John wrote, "Unless one is born of water and the Spirit, he cannot enter into the kingdom of God" (John 3:5).

What begins with the Spirit must continue with the Spirit. It is through the Spirit that Christian character is developed. It is through the Spirit that we are empowered for service. It is through the Spirit that we are guided and led, if we permit him to do so. It is through the Spirit that we are convicted of sin and constantly pointed afresh to the Savior. It is through the Spirit that we experience the mystic presence of Christ and the abundant life that he has promised. It is when the Spirit controls our lives that there can be the qualities of joy, peace, and harmony of which the Gospel of John speaks. It is also through allowing the Spirit to control our lives that we can bear the fruit of which John 15 speaks. It would seem that to abide in Christ and to be led by the Spirit would be practically synonymous expressions. Through the Spirit we become believers, and through the Spirit also we become fruitful servants of our Lord. Such life in the Spirit will be a progressive life. There will be growth and development, progress and movement rather than stagnation or regression. There will need to be a death to self, and this will not need to take place only once, but many times. Whenever Christ is no longer the center of our lives, we will need to return again to the place of self-surrender to his will. The lordship of Christ will be the first and clearest evidence of a Spirit-filled life. As we walk in the Spirit, we will develop a sensitivity to the will of God, a growing capacity to perceive opportunities for service and possibilities of ministry.

The Holy Spirit

Our blest Redeemer, ere He breathed
His tender last farewell,
A Guide, a Comforter bequeathed,
With us to dwell.

And every virtue we possess,
And every victory won,
And every thought of holiness
Are His alone.

Spirit of purity and grace,
Our weakness pitying see;
O make our hearts Thy dwelling-place,
And worthier Thee.[3]

We can no more live healthy and productive Christian lives without the Spirit than we can survive without oxygen. On jet airplanes special oxygen masks are in compartments above every seat, to be used if there should be a sudden drop in cabin pressure with a consequent loss of oxygen. This special source of oxygen is provided to insure health and life in the event of an emergency.

When the astronauts landed on the moon and went on their explorations of the lunar surface, they had to take with them their own life-support systems. In that environment persons cannot survive without them. As Christians the Spirit not only gives us life but also sustains and supports us in an environment which is often not only not encouraging to spiritual growth but also actually often hostile to it. The "world" will hate the Christian (John 15:18-19). The Spirit, however, continues to be our constant and sufficient guide (16:13).

Through the Spirit we can be effective witnesses for God. Notice how the witness of the Spirit and the witness of the believer are presented together (see 15:26-27). The Spirit often fulfills his witness through people who are yielded to him. The Spirit, in other words, helps us in our attempts at service and ministry. God is a God of variety. No snowflake and no person is exactly like another. Each has a touch of individuality upon it from the hand of the Creator. We each have our individual gifts. If we are faithful in the exercising of the gifts God has given us, then Christ by the power of the Holy Spirit can make our lives fruitful and enriching to others to the glory of God.

Veni, Creator Spiritus

Creator Spirit, by whose aid
The World's foundations first were laid,
Come, visit every pious mind;
Come, pour Thy joys on human kind;
From sin and sorrow set us free,
And make Thy temples worthy Thee.[4]

Jesus' High Priestly Prayer (17:1-26)

This chapter has often been given the above title. This chapter tells us the meaning of "eternal life," namely, "to know God," that is, to enter into fellowship and communion with him. This chapter also stresses the unity of the church (17:20-23). John 17 is certainly a high point in John and in all of Scripture. Walter Lüthi, a Lutheran pastor in Bern, Switzerland, once compared John to the highest mountain in his country. It soars above all surrounding peaks in its portrayal of the closeness which exists between the Father and the Son and in its exhortation to believers to strive for that unity which God intends for his church.

This chapter divides into three parts:

1. Jesus prays for himself (17:1-5).
2. Jesus prays for his disciples (17:6-19).
3. Jesus prays for future believers (17:20-26).

Jesus prays that he may be glorified. In John the cross is presented as the moment of glory (see 12:23-24). The cross is glory because it demonstrates God's love for us. The cross is glory because through it Jesus draws all persons to himself. The cross is glory because it makes possible humankind's reconciliation with God. The cross is glory because it gives evidence of Jesus' total obedience to the Father.

As Jesus prays for his disciples, he prays for their unity (17:11). He prays that they may be kept from the evil one (17:15). He prays that they may be "sanctified" (17:17). This means that he desires that they may be separated unto God in obedience and for service. "Sanctification" is another word for "consecration." God has been put first in their lives. Finally, Jesus prays for their mission as he sends them out into the world (17:18).

As Jesus prays for future believers, he also prays for their unity (17:20-21). He prays that the world may believe through them (17:21). He concludes by praying that these future believers may be with Jesus to behold his glory (17:24). This is the future hope of the Christian church.

As we look at this prayer, we recognize that it continues to serve as a means for instructing the disciples. It is part of the sermonic farewell discourse. In many ways we can see in the prayer a kind of summary of the message of the Gospel According to John, for it tells us who Jesus is, why he came into the world, what he has done for believers, what is expected of his disciples, and what their ultimate destiny is to be.

Believers will fulfill their mission in the world when their lives reveal the living Christ and they thus represent Jesus to the world. In the meantime their relationship within the church will be one of love and unity. The end result will be that the world will believe.

9

Life Through Death

Jim Elliot was a missionary to the Auca Indians of Ecuador. His exciting story is told by his wife, Elisabeth Elliot, in the book *Shadow of the Almighty*.[1] Jim was one of five missionaries who determined to make contact with a mysterious, almost legendary Indian tribe that lived in the depths of the Amazon jungle. Although they were successful in reaching the outskirts of the tribal area, all five were killed. The widows of the five martyrs did not regard their husbands' deaths as all in vain. Through their continued efforts, the tribe was finally reached and friendly relations established. Here is an example of victory in defeat. Jim's life was not given in vain. Through his martyrdom, and that of his colleagues, the love of God was shared with a forgotten and hidden people. The wives also demonstrated the same kind of triumph over tragedy. They did not allow the seemingly senseless killings to embitter them. They surmounted their natural feelings of hatred and revenge and demonstrated love and forgiveness to a people they had not yet met. Thereafter some of them were able to show it in person by living among the Indians and sharing their life in the jungle. They did it all in order to witness to their faith in God through Jesus Christ their Lord.

At first glance Jesus was a failure. He was put to death by his

115

enemies and deserted by most of his friends. But by his death life entered the world. By his crucifixion the forgiveness and love of God became real in a new way. Jesus had predicted that through his death life would come. He said, "The hour has come for the Son of Man to be glorified. Truly, truly, I say to you, unless a grain of wheat falls into the earth and dies, it remains by itself alone; but if it dies, it bears much fruit" (John 12:23-24). Jesus was here talking about his own death. The verse goes on, however, to make a general principle which we can apply to ourselves. It reads, "He who loves his life loses it; and he who hates his life in this world shall keep it to life eternal. If any one serves Me, let him follow Me . . ." (John 12:25-26). Jesus not only became our Savior through Calvary, but he also set for us an example of a totally unselfish life dedicated to the will of God. His disciples are challenged to follow him by the same self-denial and obedience.

In this chapter which is entitled "Life Through Death," we shall look at the account of the betrayal, trial, and death of Jesus (18:1–19:42). From seeming defeat there came victory. Out of death there came life, not only for Jesus, but also for the world. As Jesus said, "Truly, truly, I say to you, he who hears My word, and believes Him who sent Me, has eternal life, and does not come into judgment, but has passed out of death into life" (5:24).

William Tyndale was born in England around 1495. He received his B.A. and M.A. from Oxford and later studied Greek at Cambridge. He had a gift for learning languages. He became concerned that the common people did not have the Bible available in their own language. When he discussed this with a learned colleague, he got the reply that other laws were more important than God's laws. To this Tyndale answered, "If God spare my life, ere many years I will cause a boy that driveth the plough shall know more scripture than thou dost."[2] Because of opposition in England, he went to the continent of Europe and studied for a time under Martin Luther at Wittenberg. He then produced his New Testament translation which was smuggled into England by ship in sacks of grain, cloth, and fur. While living in Antwerp, he was treacherously kidnapped on May 21, 1535, and imprisoned in a fortress near Brussels. On October 6, 1536, he was strangled at the stake and his body burned in the prison yard. His devotion to the cause of God cost him his life. But through his dedication countless millions have had lives enriched through a fuller understanding of the Word of God. Like Jesus, his Master, William Tyndale is an example of one who was "victorious in defeat."

The Arrest and Trial of Jesus

In John's account of Jesus' arrest and trial there are two major divisions:

1. the interrogation by the Jewish authorities, namely, Annas and Caiaphas (pronounced: Kay' e fes) (18:1-27);
2. the trial by Pilate (18:28-19:16).

In the arrest and trial of Jesus, there appears to be a definite emphasis upon the initiative as coming from the Jewish religious authorities. Pressure is put on Pilate to render a verdict of guilty. See especially 19:12.

In John's account, there is a distinct stress upon the sovereignty and majesty of Jesus. His arrest and trial are permitted by God, but at no point is Jesus presented as being simply at the mercy of the hands of wicked men. Note how Jesus says: "You would have no authority over Me, unless it had been given you from above . . ." (19:11). A divine plan and timetable are being followed throughout. Hence what appears at first glance to be tragedy and defeat is, in the mind of the writer, clearly triumph and victory.

Annas and Caiaphas

Annas is mentioned in Luke 3:2; John 18:13, 24; and Acts 4:6. Caiaphas is spoken of in Matthew 26:3, 57; Luke 3:2; John 11:49; 18:13, 14, 24, 28; and Acts 4:6. Who were these two men before whom Jesus was questioned? Annas was appointed a high priest by Quirinius (Cyrenius), the Roman governor of Syria, in A.D. 6 or 7. He was deposed by the Roman Valerius Gratus in A.D. 15, who subsequently appointed Caiaphas as high priest. John tells us that Annas was the father-in-law of Caiaphas. The suggestion has been made that the questioning of Jesus before Annas can be compared to a kind of police interrogation of a newly arrested person before any formal trial or hearing takes place.

The trial before the Sanhedrin followed this interrogation, according to the Synoptic accounts (Matthew 26:57-66; Mark 14:53-64; Luke 22:54, 66–23:1). John simply tells us that Jesus was sent bound to Caiaphas, but he does not report a trial. All four Gospels agree that after Jesus stood before Caiaphas, he was led to Pilate. The questioning before Annas, then, was informal and unofficial. It was followed by a formal hearing which is hinted at in John 18:24, 28 but only described by the Synoptic Gospels. This formal hearing took place before the Sanhedrin and Caiaphas. It was followed by the trial before Pilate. Caiaphas and the Sanhedrin represented the Jewish authorities in Jerusalem while Pilate represented the Roman officials.

The Praetorium

According to John 18:28, Jesus was led from the house of Caiaphas to the Praetorium (KJV, "the hall of judgment"). This was the governor's official residence. It is still debated whether this is to be identified with the palace of Herod in the western part of the city of Jerusalem or with the fortress Antonia which was located northwest and immediately adjacent to the temple area.

There remains to this day a large Roman pavement where the fortress Antonia once stood. In Jerusalem it is part of the property belonging to the Convent of the Sisters of Zion. It can be seen by visitors to the Holy City. Grooves in the pavement were made in ancient times to prevent horses from slipping on the smooth surface of the large stones. It is estimated that its original size was some twenty-three hundred square yards. The massive paving blocks which can still be seen are more than a yard square and a foot thick.

The governor of Judea, Pontius Pilate, had his main residence in Caesarea, the seaport on the Mediterranean. It was here that an inscription giving his name was first found in 1961.

John's Gospel seems to minimize Pilate's involvement in Jesus' death. It appears that he was reluctantly pushed to his decision to crucify Jesus. The one thing which should not emerge from this lesson is an anti-Semitic thrust. Hardness of heart, fear, blindness, sin, the self-centeredness of persons—these factors led to the crucifixion of Jesus. No racial prejudice should emerge from a lesson such as this. Each person stands before God as an individual, and we must remember that all of Jesus' early followers were Jews! How foolish, then, to support an anti-Semitic bias on the basis of the crucifixion account. John is the Gospel, above all others, which stresses that God loves the world, not just a part of it. The Good News is for all persons.

"You are the King of the Jews?" (18:33)

The concept of the "kingdom of God" is central in the teachings of Jesus. It receives much more emphasis, however, in Matthew, Mark, and Luke than in John. It may be that the term tended to be less used at the time and in the place that John was writing. Jesus talks about his kingdom in John 18:36. There he says that it is "not of this world." What does Jesus mean by the term "kingdom"? It refers primarily to "rule, reign, sovereignty." The lordship of Christ is what is implied here. We enter the kingdom by the birth from above which comes through the Holy Spirit (3:3, 5). At that point we acknowledge the lordship of Christ over our lives and submit to his control and guidance. Jesus accepts the title "king" (18:37), but he interprets it not in relation to political power but to bearing witness to the truth. It was for this purpose that he came into the world. In the coming of Christ his kingdom was inaugurated. Not everyone acknowledged him then, and many do not confess his name now. Scripture looks forward, however, to the day when every knee shall bow to Christ and every tongue confess him as Lord (Philippians 2:10-11). Then the kingdom once inaugurated will be consummated and fully realized. In John 1:49 Nathanael said, "Rabbi, You are the Son of God; You are the King of Israel." We should regard all these titles as messianic ones. Jesus came as the One promised by the prophets of Israel. He came first to the Jewish people and then, by the grace of God, to all persons. The universal nature of Christ's redemption is well expressed in the hymn of redemption found in Revelation 5:9-10 which reads, ". . . Thou wast slain, and didst purchase for God with Thy blood men from every tribe and tongue and people and nation. And Thou hast made them to be a kingdom and priests to our God; and they will reign upon the earth."

Jesus did not suggest that his kingdom or kingship is otherworldly in the sense that it is unrelated to this world and does not affect this world's values or how his followers live in this world. He did deny, however, that his kingdom belongs to this world. Like Jesus himself, his kingdom comes from above. It belongs to the sphere of the Spirit, not to the sphere of the flesh. It is from God that it derives its origin, authority, nature, and values.

The answer of Jesus could allow Pilate to relax about Jesus' being any political threat to him. At the same time the matter of "truth" can be an even more penetrating and unnerving challenge. Pilate became the one who was, in a sense, on trial. Would he recognize the truth, and, if so, how would he respond to it? Pilate's reply, "What is truth?" suggests that while he had ceased to worry about Jesus' political ambitions, he had not gone so far as to accept his religious claims either. Pilate failed to recognize the truth in Jesus, and his rhetorical question was an indirect rejection, it would appear, of the affirmation of the Gospel of John that Jesus is "the way, and the truth, and the life" (John 14:6).

"We have a law, and by that law He ought to die because He made Himself out to be the Son of God" (19:7)

This passage is probably referring to the Jewish law against blasphemy, as found in Leviticus 24:16 which reads, "Moreover, the one who blasphemes the name of the Lord shall surely be put to death; all the congregation shall certainly stone him. The alien as well as the native, when he blasphemes the Name, shall be put to death." John 10:36 associates the claim to be God's Son with blasphemy.

Pilate's fear, as mentioned in 19:8, may have stemmed from superstition (compare Matthew 27:19); he may have thought that Jesus had magical powers. His fear may also have been politically based, namely, that he could be accused before his superiors in Rome of not properly respecting the local religious practices as he was charged to do. It was probably the former.

"He entered into the Praetorium again" (19:9)

In verse 4 Pilate brought Jesus out to the people, but it appears that he had Jesus taken back into the building again when the crowd became unruly. When Jesus was questioned further, he remained silent. In Matthew, Mark, and Luke Jesus is silent throughout the whole trial except to the question about his being king. In John the silence is temporary, for he speaks again before Pilate in verse 11. It is clear that Jesus made no effort at self-defense. He had committed himself fully to the will of the Father. Nothing could happen to him apart from the Father's will (19:11). The motif of the silence of the Messiah before his accusers is stressed in the picture of the Suffering Servant as found in Isaiah 53:7b:

> Like a lamb that is led to slaughter,
> And like a sheep that is silent before its shearers,
> So He did not open His mouth.

"He who delivered Me up to you has the greater sin" (19:11)

While this could refer to Judas, a number of interpreters favor the view that it is Caiaphas who is meant. Pilate was acting in an official capacity and was in less of a position to be well informed on religious matters than was Caiaphas. Caiaphas should have known better. Consequently, his guilt is the greater.

The Cross

In John the cross is presented as an event which took place according to the foreknowledge, plan, and timetable of God. Christ laid down his life in order that he might take it again. No one took it from him. God is sovereign and Jesus as the Son of God is not under the control of persons. The idea of the cross is frequently spoken of by the distinctive Johannine terminology "the hour" or "my hour." This expression is found in the following passages: John 2:4; 4:21, 23; 5:25, 28; 7:30; 8:20; 12:23, 27; 13:1; 16:21, 32; and 17:1. The expression "My time" is used in the same sense in 7:6, 8. The hour of the cross is the hour of Christ's glorification (7:39; 12:16, 23, 24, 28; 13:31; and 17:1).

In the Synoptic Gospels Jesus speaks of the exaltation to a throne of power and glory after his death; from that throne he will come to judge the world (Matthew 24:30-31; 25:31). In the Gospel of John, however, the sufferings and death *are* the glorification and not just preliminary to it. The reason this is so is that the cross is the complete manifestation of the goodness and love of God who loved us to the uttermost, sparing not his only Son. Glory is God in action through Jesus Christ in which the full measure of God's love is brought to bear upon the deep sin and desperate need of humankind. Here the riches of the grace of God are forever made known to humankind. Jesus dies as the Son of God but also as the obedient servant who had come not to do his own will but the will of the Father. The cross is the commencement of the glorious exaltation. It is followed by the resurrection and the giving of the promised Paraclete (Holy Spirit).

Golgotha

The location of Golgotha remains a disputed point. Since the fourth century the traditional site of both the crucifixion and the tomb in which Jesus was laid had been the area now covered by the Church of the Holy Sepulcher. Since we are told that Jesus was crucified "near the city" (John 19:20) and since Jews did not permit graveyards within the city, it is clear that both places must have been outside the walls of the ancient city. The Church of the Holy Sepulcher is within the present city wall. Those who maintain the authenticity of the tradition that this is the place where Jesus was crucified theorize that the ancient city wall ran south of the present wall. In Jesus' day, therefore, this place would have been outside the city. Further excavation is taking place now in Jerusalem, and it is hoped that evidence will be forthcoming to resolve this disputed point. Another possible site which has been suggested is "Gordon's Calvary," which lies outside the present city walls. Here there is an empty tomb and in front of it a groove where a round stone could have been rolled to cover the entrance. Certainly the setting of this spot in the middle of a quiet garden and away from the noise and bustle of the surrounding city is a better place to envision what the place was like in the first century. The tradition that this is the place of crucifixion and burial is only about a century old. Quite apart from whether or not it is, the merits of the place are that it recreates the first-century situation much better than the massive old church setting, in the Church of the Sepulcher, which marks the spot where Jesus was supposed to have been crucified.

"He went out, bearing His own cross" (19:17)

What Jesus carried was probably the crosspiece, or transverse beam, since the upright wood, which above ground was about nine feet in length, was generally left standing in the place of execution. It would have been used at more than one crucifixion. Mark and Matthew indicate that Simon of Cyrene helped Jesus to bear this beam. It may be that Jesus was so weakened by the scourging (which was a very severe form of punishment) that he could not carry it. They went to a location identified as "the place of a skull." The Hebrew word is *Gulgolet* and the Aramaic *Gulgolta,* meaning "skull, cranium." In the Latin Vulgate translation in Mark 15:22 the Latin word *calvaria,* meaning "skull," is used. From this word we get the English place name "Calvary." The only place where the word "Calvary" appears in the King James Version is in Luke 23:33. There it is just a rendering of the Greek word *kranion,* meaning "skull." The KJV translators were obviously influenced by the Latin Vulgate in introducing the place name "Calvary." Modern hymns have popularized this name.

There They Crucified Him (19:18)

Josephus called crucifixion "the most wretched of deaths"; and Cicero spoke of it as a "most cruel and terrible penalty." Consider the love, commitment, and dedication of our Savior! Our redemption cost an awful price!

"Pilate wrote an inscription also, and put it on the cross. And it was written, 'JESUS THE NAZARENE, THE KING OF THE JEWS'" (19:19)

All the Gospels mention an inscription, but only John attributes it to Pilate's order. This placard was not uncommon. It usually bore either the name of the condemned person or the nature of his crime or both. The wording of the inscription varies in all four Gospels. It is clear that some measure of freedom is felt in reporting details like this. The main ideas are the same in either case. The variation is as follows:

Matthew 27:37—"THIS IS JESUS THE KING OF THE JEWS."
Mark 15:26— "THE KING OF THE JEWS."
Luke 23:38— "THIS IS THE KING OF THE JEWS."
John 19:19— "JESUS THE NAZARENE, THE KING OF THE JEWS."

Only John mentions the languages of the inscription. The stress on the three languages is certainly in keeping with the universal thrust of this Gospel. It echoes again the concern expressed by the Samaritan villagers when they said, "It is no longer because of what you said that we believe, for we have heard for ourselves and know that this One is indeed the Savior of the world" (4:42).

They Took His Garments (19:23)

This has reference to outer garments. In Roman practice the soldiers had a right to take the prisoners' clothes for themselves. These they divided by casting lots for them.

"Jesus, knowing that all things had already been accomplished" (19:28)

John relates the finishing of Jesus' work and life to the completion of God's preordained plan. The same idea is present when Jesus says in verse 30, "It is finished!" John is not thinking only about Jesus' death. He views what is happening as the completion of God's plan of salvation for the world. Jesus has completed his appointed task. He has done so successfully. Now wholeness and salvation have been made possible for all persons. Wholeness and salvation have come through Jesus Christ. Wholeness and salvation have been consummated at the cross.

"Because it was the day of preparation" (19:31)

This would refer to the period of time from 6 P.M. Thursday to about 6 P.M. Friday when the sabbath would begin. That sabbath was very holy (a high day) because it fell on the Passover.

"One of the soldiers pierced His side with a spear, and immediately there came out blood and water" (19:34)

This seems to have a double meaning for John. The first and obvious meaning is that Jesus was already dead. Along with this idea, however, there is the implied affirmation that Jesus died a real death. His body was a real body. There were some around when John was writing who maintained that Jesus did not have a body of flesh and blood. He only appeared to have a human body, they said. They argued that his body resembled our bodies but was of a different substance. This theory maintained that all flesh and all matter are inherently evil. Therefore, they held that Jesus who was the Son of God could not really have had a human body. This theory was called Docetism (from the Greek word *dokeo,* meaning "to seem," "to appear"). The church later condemned this theory as a heresy. Long before it was taken up in the church councils, however, John rejected it. He also attacks it in John 1:14 ("the Word became flesh") and in 1 John 4:2-3 and 2 John, verse 7.

"NOT A BONE OF HIM SHALL BE BROKEN" (19:36)

It is clear that Jesus is being compared to the paschal lamb. Of the lamb we read, "You shall not break a bone of it" (Exodus 12:46, RSV). Paul makes the same comparison when he writes, "For Christ our Passover also has been sacrificed" (1 Corinthians 5:7*b*).

The Cross as the Way of Love

Jesus demonstrated the way of love. He attacked that which was wrong in his day, but he did so in a nonviolent manner. He who lived nonviolently died a violent death. The same was true of Mahatma Gandhi and of Martin Luther King.

Gandhi lived for some years in South Africa where he was a lawyer. He fought against the racial injustice he experienced there by fighting legislation directed against his race. He never claimed to be a Christian as such. He was a Hindu. He asserted the unity of humankind under one God, and throughout his life he preached from the Christian and Moslem Scriptures as well as from the Hindu sacred writings. He once said that along with the Hindu Scriptures, that which most influenced his life was the Sermon on the Mount. He struggled for the independence of India from British control, and to do so he organized several nonviolent resistance campaigns. On January 30, 1948, while holding a prayer and pacification meeting in New Delhi in order to ease tensions between Hindus and Moslems, he was shot and killed by a Hindu. His ashes were deposited in the Ganges River. On this occasion the Indian government swore to uphold his ideals. Would you say that Gandhi was a failure? Or would it be true of him also that at least in some measure he, like Jesus, was victorious in death?

In the case of Christ we see in his death the provision for eternal salvation. But we must also see the total commitment of Jesus, the man, to the will of the Father, to the ideals he taught, to the cause to which he had dedicated himself. We should be able to identify with these things. We must not minimize the deity of the Christ, but at the same time we must not repeat the heresy of the Gnostics who said that Jesus did not really have a human body.

By making Jesus so different from ourselves, we may consciously or unconsciously be removing his life from being a direct challenge to us. We may be saying, "But he was the Son of God. You can't expect other people to have this kind of dedication! He was different from other men and women." True, he was. His life remains, however, as an example of total commitment to the will of God. We cannot escape that fact, and we cannot escape the challenge which he gave to his disciples when he said to them, "Follow me." We are to follow him not only as a person, but we are also to follow (to the best of our ability and with the help of God) the ideals and the life-style which Jesus of Nazareth demonstrated. His life-style was costly. It led to the cross. Is that costly part of the gospel message preached and heard by us along with John 3:16 about the love of God for us?

Life Proclaimed

The Resurrection of Jesus (20:1-29)

The joyous Easter greeting "He is risen!" with its answer "He is risen indeed!" carries with it the essence of the Good News concerning Jesus Christ. This was the climax of the life and ministry of Jesus. While it came at the end of Jesus' life on earth and is the fact reported at the conclusion of the accounts of Jesus' life as given in the Gospels, we would be in serious error if we were to view it as a dispensable addition to an otherwise wonderful story. The resurrection of Jesus is too much a part of the very fabric of the Good News concerning Christ for it to be removed without tearing the garment of witness beyond repair. To put it another way, this affirmation is so central to the message of the apostles that it can be compared to the foundation of a building. The Gospels would never have been written, and the early disciples would never have risked both reputation and life itself to tell their stories, if it were not for their conviction that Jesus Christ is Lord, and that this fact had been demonstrated by the resurrection of Jesus from the dead. They viewed it as God's seal upon his life and person.

Mary Magdalene's Great Discovery (20:1)

In the accounts given in the Synoptic Gospels Mary Magdalene is accompanied by several other women on the occasion when she discovers that the tomb is empty (Matthew 28:1-10; Mark 16:1-8; Luke 24:1-11). For some unknown reason John mentions only Mary Magdalene. Perhaps this is because he plans to place emphasis upon the personal appearance which Jesus makes to her in the following narrative (20:11-18). It is most unlikely that Mary would have gone alone in the dark to a place of execution and a graveyard located outside the city of Jerusalem. For John's purpose the presence of the other women was not important for the story he wants to tell.

Mary went to the tomb early while it was still dark. The time is generally interpreted to have been during what was called the fourth watch of the night, which went from 3 A.M. to 6 A.M. While the Gospel According to Luke introduces Mary Magdalene fairly early into the story of Jesus (see Luke 8:2-3), the other Gospels mention her by name only during the last week of the ministry of Jesus. John has included her in his list of the women who were at the cross (John 19:25). This is the only previous mention of her in this Gospel. She is presented as the first witness of the empty tomb. While the other Gospel writers mention other women who accompanied Mary Magdalene when this discovery was made, it is to be noted that Mary's name is always mentioned first. Mary ran and told Peter and "the other disciple whom Jesus loved" what she had discovered. She said, "They have taken away the Lord out of the tomb, and we do not know where they have laid Him" (20:2). By adding the words "we do not know," we have indirect support for our conclusion that Mary was not alone when this discovery of the empty tomb was made.

We can only surmise why the second disciple mentioned above is not actually named. A traditional interpretation is that it has reference to the disciple whose testimony stands behind this Gospel narrative. If so, we presume that the phrase "the disciple whom Jesus loved" was a term given to the author by the Christian community that loved him and preserved his witness to Jesus. It is difficult to view the title as one which a disciple would use of himself. That would suggest an improper arrogance and lack of humility. If given to him by others, it can be seen as a touching testimonial to the warmth with which the disciple was held in the hearts of the members of the community of faith in which he ministered.

The Two Disciples (20:2-8)

Simon Peter and the beloved disciple ran to the tomb and found that what Mary had told them was true. The result of their discovery was faith (20:8). The emphasis here on faith is probably intended as part of the Gospel's appeal to the readers also to believe. Compare 20:26-28 where Thomas comes to faith as well.

Mary Magdalene Meets Jesus (20:11-18)

Mary saw Jesus but at first did not recognize either his form or his voice (20:14-15). When Jesus spoke her name, however, she suddenly knew that the one before her was her Lord (20:16). It has been suggested that this moving account of Jesus speaking the name of Mary is intended to remind the readers of the reassurance which Jesus had spoken earlier in the Gospel when he said, "He calls his own sheep by name" (10:3).

Mary replied with the single Aramaic word "Rabboni!" which the author interprets as "Teacher." Literally, it means, "my Teacher." The same term occurs in Mark 10:51. It is simply another form of the word "Rabbi," and it is translated in the same way. (See John 1:38.) In the New Testament "Rabbi" is an honorary title. It does not imply any official appointment or recognition. It is a title of respect given to religious leaders and teachers.

Jesus then says to Mary, "Stop clinging to Me" (20:17a). It is best rendered in this way rather than in the manner of the older translation: "Touch me not" (KJV). The present imperative used in a prohibition, as here, implies the stopping of an action which has already begun. Recognizing this fact removes the seeming difficulty which appears when later in this chapter Jesus urges Thomas to touch him (20:27). The concern of Jesus apparently is not whether or not Mary touches him, but he needs to remind her that he will no longer be with her, and with the others, as he had been with them before his crucifixion. He will be with them in spirit—in fact, through the Holy Spirit (see 14:23; 20:22)—but not in body. It is this truth which Mary has yet to learn. Jesus did not return to this temporal world with all of its limitations and restrictions. He had been raised in glory, and in this new state he was released into the world to be the Lord of the church. For a short time he appeared to his disciples, but then he ascended to the Father and is thereafter present to the church through the Holy Spirit who makes the presence of Jesus real to his followers.

Mary returned with a message which can in some measure be the message of every believer who encounters the risen Jesus. She said simply and clearly, "I have seen the Lord" (20:18). Jesus is alive. Death has not held him. He has risen.

"Jesus came and stood in their midst and said to them, 'Peace be with you'" (20:19)

The word "peace" can mean many things. It can mean:

1. a pact or agreement to end hostilities,
2. a state of public tranquillity or quiet,
3. harmony in human or personal relations,
4. the fuller and richer meaning as found in the Old Testament where it refers to a state of wholeness. This may refer to physical health, to prosperity, security from danger, or to spiritual completeness. The Hebrew word for this is, of course, "shalom." It is a beautiful word. It can be used in modern Hebrew simply to say "hello" or "good-bye." But it can have a much deeper meaning.

Jesus greeted the disciples three times after the resurrection with the salutation, "Peace be with you" (20:19, 21, 26). Through Christ "peace" has come. Listen to the words of Paul: "Therefore having been justified by faith, we have peace with God through our Lord Jesus Christ" (Romans 5:1). "AND HE CAME AND PREACHED PEACE TO YOU WHO WERE FAR AWAY, AND PEACE TO THOSE WHO WERE NEAR; for through Him we both have our access in one Spirit to the Father" (Ephesians 2:17-18).

"As the Father has sent Me, I also send you" (20:21b)

This statement may be compared to the Great Commission as found in Matthew 28:19-20. It picks up the missionary theme expressed earlier (John 4:35-38; 15:27). John is in many ways a missionary book. It is much concerned with the outreach and expansion of the gospel.

"And when He had said this, He breathed on them, and said to them, 'Receive the Holy Spirit'" (20:22)

This calls to mind the account of Pentecost as given in the book of Acts. John states here that the Holy Spirit is given by Jesus Christ. This is an important theme in John (see 7:38-39; 15:26). The use of the verb "he breathed on them" appears to be selected on the basis of the expression found at creation, "Then the LORD God formed man of dust from the ground, and breathed into his nostrils the breath of life; and man became a living being" (Genesis 2:7). John is thinking of a new quality of life which comes only through the Holy Spirit. As believers, we share in God's new creation.

"If you forgive the sins of any, their sins have been forgiven them; if you retain the sins of any, they have been retained" (20:23)

This verse, along with others like it in the Synoptics, has been abused. It has been interpreted to mean that the church can determine a person's salvation by the act of some official in the church. Clearly God does not give this kind of authority to us. However, the gospel message is given to the church. In the faithful proclamation of that word we make possible the salvation of the world. We can affirm with confidence that anyone who receives the Good News of Jesus Christ by faith can have the assurance of sins forgiven. Anyone who rejects the Good News can be firmly warned that apart from the Christ there is no salvation. The church becomes the channel of salvation but certainly not the source of it. When I speak of the church, I am thinking not so much of the institution as I am of the body of believers who comprise the church. To each of us comes the responsibility of sharing the Good News.

"Thomas answered and said to Him, 'My Lord and my God!'" (20:28)

This is the climactic confession of the Gospel of John. It is the one toward which all the others have been pointing. By implication, it is the confession that the author endorses and which he desires that all the readers will be willing to affirm.

Jesus replied to Thomas, "Because you have seen Me, have you believed? Blessed are they who did not see, and yet believed" (20:29). As the writer of John's Gospel includes these words, who can he have in mind except the readers for whom he writes? They are the ones who will not have had the opportunity given to Thomas. They should not on this account feel themselves disadvantaged. It is even more blessed, says Jesus, to come to Thomas's faith and confession without this special, direct meeting with Jesus. These words, of course, can apply with equal validity and force to the twentieth-century reader of the Gospel According to John.

The Statement of Purpose (20:30-31)

John's statement of purpose really brings the Gospel According to

John to a close. He tells us that he wrote in order that his readers might find "life." This, he says, will be theirs through believing in Jesus as the Christ, the Son of God. It is for this reason that he has written his entire Gospel. He has given us an account of the resurrection of Jesus, of his appearances, of his gift of the Spirit, and of his commissioning of the disciples to their missionary task. That really completes the story. There is, however, a twenty-first chapter to this Gospel. This chapter appears to be an afterthought, written to meet some new needs which had arisen after the completion of the earlier chapters.

The Epilogue (John 21)

Scholars continue to debate whether or not the same person who wrote John 1–20 also wrote John 21. Various suggestions have also been made as to why this chapter was added. Some surmise that it was to stress the reality of the bodily resurrection of Jesus, thereby opposing the heresy that Jesus did not really experience a literal resurrection of the body which had been placed in the tomb. Others advance the thought that this chapter was penned in order to resolve the tension which had arisen because of the unexpected death of the "beloved disciple" (21:20-23). The prominence given to Peter in this chapter, who three times confesses his faith in Jesus, in contrast to his earlier triple denial, may suggest yet another reason why this epilogue was added. It may have been the writer's way of affirming that Peter was fully reinstated to favor and responsibility in the Christian community by Jesus himself.

Jesus Appears to the Disciples as They Fish (21:1-14)

The narrative of Jesus appearing to the disciples as they are fishing is very reminiscent of a similar account found in Luke 5:4-11. There, too, the instruction of Jesus, as to where to let down the net, led to a full catch. It is clear that in both instances the real issue at hand is not literal fishing. What is behind the narrative is a concern for evangelism. The net is the gospel, and the fish are men and women who become followers of Jesus. This is why in the account in Luke the incident ends with Jesus' statement, "Do not fear, from now on you will be catching men" (Luke 5:10).

Perhaps this incident is told with the implied suggestion that to labor without Jesus is to labor in vain. He had said to them earlier, "Apart from Me you can do nothing" (John 15:5b). Effective evangelism can only be carried out when we labor both in the name and in the power of our risen Lord.

The Recommissioning of Peter (21:15-17)

Peter confesses his love for Jesus in this section, and Jesus commissions him three times to care for the "sheep," that is, the followers of Jesus. Many sermons have been preached on the fact that two different words for love occur in these verses, namely, "phileo" and "agapao." When a study is made of John's use of these words elsewhere in the Gospel, however, we find that he uses them interchangeably. It is probably safer, therefore, not to seek to find any subtle distinction between the uses of these two words in this dialogue. Both words appear to be synonymous in meaning in the context here.

Self-Denial Versus Self-Love

Looking at Peter, and seeing how he had three times denied his Lord, reminds us that we, too, are always in danger of turning back from the full implications of discipleship. We need constantly to abide in Christ if we are to endure the temptations of the world. Much of "the world" and its values are not external to us but are a part of the "old self" within. Constant vigilance, with the strength that the Spirit gives, is the best protection against the temptation to deny by word or by life the Lord in whom we have placed our trust.

The resurrection of Jesus Christ becomes symbolic of the new life to which we, too, have been raised. Christ was victorious in death. In a death to sin and selfishness we, too, can experience the joyous victory of the freedom which has become ours through becoming disciples of Jesus. We, too, have been liberated in order that, like Peter, we might serve in the name of Jesus Christ our Lord.

The Predicted Deaths of Peter and the Beloved Disciple (21:18-23)

Since the deaths of both disciples are spoken of here, it may well be that John 21 was written after both of these deaths had taken place. Peter, we believe, was martyred several decades before this writing of chapter 21. The beloved disciple may have died more recently. Some, however, expected him to live until Jesus returned. This, the writer of the epilogue says, stemmed from a misinterpretation of the actual words that Jesus had said about him (21:23). The verses may then have been added to correct this error and to calm the hearts of some who had begun to have doubts about Jesus and his messiahship because of this misunderstanding.

The Endorsement and Close (21:24-25)

The community of faith expresses its stamp of approval on what has been written as having come from the preaching and teaching of the beloved disciple (21:24). The plural is used: "we know." The Christian community which is gathered around John is eager to endorse that what has been recorded is faithful and true and can be relied upon as a basis for faith and trust in Jesus Christ as Lord.

A new close to the book is now penned to replace the earlier one found at 20:30-31. The writer affirms that not the half has been told that could be recorded about Jesus. The material is selective and partial. Nonetheless there is more than enough here to meet the genuine needs of every inquirer. To tell everything that Jesus did and said would be impossible. As far as the writer of this final comment is concerned, there would not be enough papyrus and ink in the world to finish the task.

God's Peace in Our Lives

One of the lessons which we may learn from the post-resurrection appearances of Jesus is that his presence brings and gives peace. Doubts and fears may be replaced in our lives by the peace of God through the encounter and daily fellowship with the risen Christ. God's peace involves reconciliation and fellowship both with God and with people.

On a trip to Israel I visited a factory which, using olive wood, makes mementos. Among those available was a wall plaque with a single Hebrew word on it: "Shalom." This word will always suggest to me all that the Bible means by "peace." I shall inevitably think of the historic benediction found in Numbers 6:24-26,

The LORD bless you, and keep you;
The LORD make His face shine on you,
And be gracious to you;
The LORD lift up His countenance on you,
And give you peace.

I shall add to this remembrance, however, the words of Jesus addressed to his disciples when, after the resurrection, he said to them, "Peace be with you" (John 20:19). It is his resurrection alone which can give us God's peace, both in this life and in the life to come.

Notes

Chapter 1. The Gospel of Life

[1] Eusebius, *Ecclesiastical History VI,* The Loeb Classical Library, trans. J.E.L. Oulton (Cambridge, Mass.: Harvard University Press, 1942), p. xiv.

[2] Leon Morris, "History and Theology in the Fourth Gospel," *Faith and Thought,* vol. 92 (1962), p. 125.

[3] This helpful outline has been suggested by Raymond E. Brown, *The Gospel According to John (I-XII),* The Anchor Bible (Garden City, N.Y.: Doubleday & Company, Inc., 1966), vol. 29, p. cxxxviii.

Chapter 2. The Word of Life

[1] Pliny, *Letters,* The Loeb Classical Library, trans. William Melmouth, rev. W. M. L. Hutchinson (Cambridge, Mass.: Harvard University Press, 1935), Book 10, p. xcvi.

[2] Martin Luther, *Commentary on Saint Paul's Epistle to the Galatians* (Grand Rapids, Mich.: Wm. B. Eerdmans Publishing Company, 1930), p. 418.

[3] Quoted in a lecture delivered at Eastern Baptist Theological Seminary, April 14, 1977.

[4] *Ibid.*

[5] Gerald Ford, "Lessons from the Presidency," *Christianity Today,* vol. 21, no. 20 (July 29, 1977), p. 19.

[6] Helmut Thielicke, *The Freedom of the Christian Man,* trans. John W. Doberstein (New York: Harper & Row, Publishers, 1963), p. 202.

[7] Hubert H. Humphrey, "You Can't Quit," *Reader's Digest,* vol. 111, no. 664 (August, 1977), pp. 58-59.

Chapter 3.   Life Through Believing

[1] Merrill C. Tenney, *John: The Gospel of Belief* (Grand Rapids, Mich.: Wm. B. Eerdmans Publishing Company, 1948).

[2] Charles W. Colson, *Born Again* (Old Tappan, N.J.: Chosen Books, Inc., 1976).

[3] Billy Graham, *How to Be Born Again* (Waco, Tex.: Word, Inc., 1977).

[4] *The Manual of Discipline,* 2,25–3,12, in Theodore H. Gaster, trans., *The Dead Sea Scriptures in English Translation* (Garden City, N.Y.: Anchor Books, imprint of Anchor Press/Doubleday & Company, Inc., 1957), pp. 47-48.

[5] William Barclay, *The Gospel of John, Volume 1,* The Daily Study Bible Series (Philadelphia: The Westminster Press, 1956), p. 119.

[6] Tenney, *op. cit.,* p. 87.

[7] George Matheson, "O Love That Wilt Not Let Me Go," in *Christian Worship* (Valley Forge: Judson Press, 1953), p. 388.

Chapter 4.   From Death to Life

[1] See T. H. Gaster, "Samaritans," in George A. Buttrick, gen. ed., *The Interpreter's Dictionary of the Bible, Volume R-Z* (Nashville: Abingdon Press, 1962), pp. 190-197.

Chapter 5.   Jesus, the Source of Life

[1] Albert Schweitzer, *The Quest of the Historical Jesus* (New York: Macmillan, Inc., 1961).

[2] Malcolm Muggeridge, *Jesus, the Man Who Lives* (New York: Harper & Row, Publishers, 1975), p. 71.

[3] _____, *Something Beautiful for God: Mother Teresa of Calcutta* (London: Collins, 1971), pp. 17-18.

Chapter 6.   Life in Fullness

[1] William Barclay, *The Gospel of John, Volume 2* (Philadelphia: The Westminster Press, 1956), p. 50.

[2] Raymond E. Brown, *The Gospel According to John (I-XII),* The Anchor Bible (Garden City, N.Y.: Doubleday & Company, Inc., 1966), vol. 29, p. 376.

[3] Horatius Bonar, "I Heard the Voice of Jesus," in James Dalton Morrison, ed., *Masterpieces of Religious Verse* (New York: Harper & Row, Publishers, 1948), p. 230.

[4] A. Guilding, *The Fourth Gospel and Jewish Worship: A Study of the Relation of St. John's Gospel to the Ancient Jewish Lectionary System* (Oxford: Clarendon Press, 1960).

[5] Leon Morris, *The Gospel According to John,* The New International Commentary on the New Testament (Grand Rapids, Mich.: Wm. B. Eerdmans Publishing Company, 1971), p. 546.

Chapter 7. Life Transformed

[1] Merrill C. Tenney, *John: The Gospel of Belief* (Grand Rapids, Mich.: Wm. B. Eerdmans Publishing Company, 1948), p. 199.

[2] Leon Morris, *The Gospel According to John,* The New International Commentary on the New Testament (Grand Rapids, Mich.: Wm. B. Eerdmans Publishing Company, 1971), p. 617.

[3] Dietrich Bonhoeffer, *The Cost of Discipleship* (New York: Macmillan, Inc., 1959), p. 79.

[4] *Ibid.,* p. 80.

[5] Walter Lüthi, *St. John's Gospel,* trans. Kurt Schoenenberger (Edinburgh and London: Oliver and Boyd, 1960), p. 180. Used by permission of John Knox Press.

[6] Raymond E. Brown, *The Gospel According to John (XIII-XXI),* The Anchor Bible (Garden City, N.Y.: Doubleday & Company, Inc., 1970), vol. 29A, p. 548.

[7] J. H. Bernard, *A Critical and Exegetical Commentary on the Gospel According to St. John, Volume 2,* ed. A. H. McNeile (Edinburgh: T. & T. Clark, 1928), p. 459.

[8] Lüthi, *op. cit.,* p. 181.

[9] Morris, *op. cit.,* p. 646.

[10] Brown, *op. cit.,* p. 636.

Chapter 8. Life in Christ

[1] Leon Morris, *The Gospel According to John,* The New International Commentary on the New Testament (Grand Rapids, Mich.: Wm. B. Eerdmans Publishing Company, 1971), p. 673.

[2] John Calvin, *Commentary on the Gospel According to John, Volume 2,* trans. William Pringle (Edinburgh: Edinburgh Printing Company, 1847), p. 108.

[3] Harriet Auber, "The Holy Spirit," in James Dalton Morrison, ed., *Masterpieces of Religious Verse* (New York: Harper & Row, Publishers, 1948), pp. 247, 248.

[4] John Dryden, "Veni, Creator Spiritus," in *ibid.,* p. 116.

Chapter 9. Life Through Death

[1] Elisabeth Elliot, *Shadow of the Almighty: The Life and Testament of Jim Elliott* (New York: Harper & Row, Publishers, 1958).

[2] S. L. Greenslade, ed., *The Cambridge History of the Bible* (Cambridge: At the University Press, 1963), pp. 141, 142.

Bibliography

Barclay, William, *The Gospel of John,* 2 vols. The Daily Study Bible Series. Philadelphia: The Westminster Press, 1956.

Barrett, C.K., *The Gospel According to St. John.* Philadelphia: The Westminster Press, 1979.

Brown, Raymond E., *The Gospel According to John.* The Anchor Bible Series, vols. 29 and 29A. Garden City, N.Y.: Doubleday & Company, Inc., 1966, 1970.

Guthrie, Donald, "John," in *The New Bible Commentary,* rev. ed. Grand Rapids, Mich.: Wm. B. Eerdmans Publishing Company, 1970, pp. 926-967.

Morris, Leon, *The Gospel of John.* The New International Commentary of the New Testament. Grand Rapids, Mich.: Wm. B. Eerdmans Publishing Company, 1970.

Tasker, R.V.G., *The Gospel According to St. John.* Grand Rapids, Mich.: Wm. B. Eerdmans Publishing Company, 1960.

Index

Subject Index

Author Index

141

Index to the Gospel According to John

Index to the Letters of John